APRICOT NUT BREAD

½ cup diced dried apricots—(soak, drain and grind)
1 egg
1 cup sugar
2 tbsp. melted butter
2 cups sifted flour
3 tsp. baking powder
¼ tsp. soda
¾ tsp. salt
½ cup strained orange juice
¼ cup water
1 cup broken walnut pieces

Beat egg, stir in sugar and butter. Mix well. Sift flour with baking powder, soda, salt. Add alternately with the orange juice and water to the sugar mixture. Add apricots and nuts.

Mix well. Bake in loaf pan in 350 degree oven for 1½ hours or until firm when tested.

CONTINENTAL SALAD

1 pkg. lemon or orange flavored gelatin
1½ cups canned grapefruit juice
1 can or jar (16 oz.) diced beets
½ cup sliced celery
salad greens

Dissolve gelatin in hot grapefruit juice and add ½ cup liquid drained from beets: chill until partially thickened--fold in drained beets and celery. Pour into large salad mold—chill until firm. Unmold on salad greens and top with Sesame Seed Dressing.

SESAME SEED DRESSING

Gradually blend 1 tbsp. canned grapefruit juice into 1 pkg. (3 oz.) cream cheese, beating until fluffy.

Fold in ¼ cup mayonnaise and 1 tbsp. toasted sesame seed.

White House recipes selected by Mrs. Richard M. Nixon

RASPBERRY PIE

2 10-ounce packages frozen raspberries, thawed
2 cups vanilla wafer crumbs
½ cup sugar
1 teaspoon cinnamon
5 tablespoons melted butter
1 envelope unflavored gelatine
¼ cup cold water
½ teaspoon lemon peel
½ pint heavy cream
1 teaspoon vanilla

Drain raspberries, reserving 1 cup of the juice. Combine crumbs, sugar, ½ teaspoon of the cinnamon and the butter; pat into a 10-inch pie plate. Bake in 375 degree oven 8 to 10 minutes; cool. Soften gelatine in water. Mix the reserve raspberry juice, the remaining ½ teaspoon cinnamon and lemon peel and heat to boiling. Remove from heat; add gelatine and stir until melted. Chill until mixture just begins to thicken. Whip cream; add vanilla. Fold raspberries, gelatine mixture and whipped cream together. Pour into pie shell. Chill. Decorate with additional whipped cream if desired. Serves 6 to 8.

BLUEBERRY DESSERT

2½ cups fresh blueberries or 2 10-ounce packages frozen unsweetened blueberries
½ cup sugar
¼ teaspoon orange peel
dash of mace
⅛ teaspoon cardamom
1 cup pie crust mix
1 tablespoon butter
2 teaspoons lemon juice
½ teaspoon vanilla

Place blueberries in buttered 1¼ quart shallow baking dish. Combine sugar, orange peel, mace and cardamom. Sprinkle sugar mixture and pie crust mix in alternate layers over blueberries. Continue until all is used. Dot with butter. Drizzle lemon juice and vanilla over all. Bake in 350 degree oven 45 minutes. Serve with whipped cream if desired. Serves 4 to 6.

The Presidents' Own

WHITE HOUSE

COOKBOOK

Compiled by

ROBERT JONES

Authentic recipes for delectable dishes enjoyed by the
Presidents and First Ladies, with interesting historical
notes on the White House, its distinguished guests, and
the excellent cuisine directed by its stewards and chefs.

CULINARY ARTS INSTITUTE

Chicago, Illinois 60616

1973

The Presidents'
Own White House Cookbook

JUST AS THE DECOR OF THE WHITE HOUSE has generally reflected the personal tastes of its First Ladies, the White House cuisine has been influenced by the preferences of the Presidents, their distinguished guests and, particularly for formal occasions, by a long line of notable stewards and White House chefs.

The recipes in *The Presidents' Own White House Cookbook* represent long years of research by its author and the invaluable cooperation of many great libraries, historical societies and knowledgeable people. Authentic recipes have been revised when necessary to meet today's culinary standards. They provide an excellent cookbook of romantic appeal and contemporary usefulness.

Some food historians contend an orphan named Amelia Simmons wrote the first American cookbook. It has a very long (47 words) title and a skimpy (46 pages) content of receipts.

Publication date was 1796. Before that date, cookbooks were reprints of English works. Hannah Glass' *The Art of Cookery Made Plain and Easy,* was a colonial favorite. There were those who maintained no woman could really cook, and that Hannah Glass was just a pseudonym for an English doctor! The other favorite guidebook of the time was *The Compleat Housewife* published by E. Smith of England.

Martha Washington's personal cookbook was a manuscript collection of receipts largely taken from the Glass and Smith books. It had been compiled and given to her by the mother of Martha's first husband. Martha, in turn, passed the book on to her granddaughter, after inscribing the flyleaf thusly: "This book written by Eleanore Parke Custis's Great Grandmother Mrs. John Custis, was given to her by her beloved Grandmother Martha Washington, formerly Mrs. Daniel Custis." The soft, leather-bound book, with its yellowed pages, is now the property of the Historical Society of Pennsylvania.

In 1824 a cookbook which had been compiled by the sister-in-law of Jefferson's daughter was published, and the inscription on the flyleaf was dedicated to her: "For Mrs. Randolph, Monticello, from her affectionate friend and sister."

Thomas Jefferson was much interested in cooking. He liked this little book so well that when it was published, he wrote his favorite recipes into it on the extra pages—in the same precise handwriting that earlier had penned the Declaration of Independence. Some recipes he had brought back from Paris, when he served as Minister Plenipotentiary to France. Some were favorite receipts of the James Monroe family. The book, owned by the James Monroe Memorial Foundation, is on display in the China Room of the White House.

Happily, the White House has been for more than 165 years the scene of elegant dining, a rich source of superlative examples of our American cuisine, the best of which have been included in these pages.

The White House is a home, the official residence of U.S. Presidents and their families. There are family meals and small, informal luncheons, and dinners at which the menu may feature the favorite dishes of the Chief Executives and the First Ladies. Many of the finest and most interesting recipes in *The Presidents' Own White House Cookbook* were enjoyed by the President whose name they bear, often brought to the White House in his wife's personal recipe file. Other recipes, not attributed to Presidents, have appeared frequently on White House menus for formal occasions.

In the search for authentic recipes, a wealth of little-known information about the White House and its occupants was discovered. You will discover something of our country's history in *The Presidents' Own White House Cookbook* as well as a treasure of new exciting recipes that will win a high place in your culinary repertoire and the hearts of your appreciative family and guests.

Copyright © 1968, 1972, 1973 by Culinary Arts Institute

Manufactured in the United States of America and published simultaneously in Canada by North American Educational Guild, Ltd., Winnipeg, Manitoba.

International Standard Book Number: 0-8326-0541-7

Rules Governing Social Procedure in Washington

For members of the government and their families, social life in Washington is of necessity governed by well-established rules. Since the general public may be less familiar with the protocol they are expected to observe, here are some things you should know if you are invited to the White House.

An invitation to the White House is considered a *must*. Your acceptance (formal, on plain white stationery; informal, on folded notepaper) should read:

> *Mr. & Mrs. John D. Smith*
> *have the honor to accept*
> *the invitation to a reception*
> *on Sunday, October twenty-second*
> *four to six o'clock*

The envelope should be addressed to your hostess. Answer dinner invitations immediately, but invitations to afternoon receptions or teas need no answer unless requested on the invitation.

What to Wear

White House state dinners and evening receptions are formal affairs at which men wear white tie and tails. Women wear long formal gowns with long white gloves or gloves made of the same material as the dress; for a daytime tea, wear a simple short afternoon dress with hat and gloves.

General Notes

Enter the White House through the east wing on East Executive Avenue, driving past the guard to the entrance door. It will be more convenient to use a cab if your car is not chauffeur driven, but parking space is reserved for guests' cars. Inside, aides are stationed to guide you to the room in which the line will form to be received by the President.

The President, Vice President, Speaker, Chief Justice, and Ambassadors are to be addressed by their titles alone, as *Mr. Speaker*. Senators are introduced as *Senator* Smith; a member of the House of Representatives is Mr. Smith of (his state).

You are free to depart any time after the President leaves.

The President's House, designed and built by James Hoban, was the first public building erected in Washington, D.C. It was occupied by John Adams in the fall of 1800 when the government moved from Philadelphia to Washington. Even though it was still unfinished, the President and his wife, Abigail, held a New Year's Reception, the first full scale social event in the White House.

Illustration Sources and Credits
Thomas Jefferson Memorial Foundation • The Pennsylvania Railroad Company
Virginia Chamber of Commerce • The New York Public Library • National Park Service
Courtesy Museum of Fine Arts, Boston (M. & M. Karolik Collection) • Smithsonian Institution
Yale University Art Gallery (Mabel Brady Garven Collection) • San Francisco Public Library
Library of Congress • Chicago Historical Society • Chicago Public Library
The Brooklyn Museum • Mount Vernon Ladies' Association • United Press International
Cover picture, Adams' tureen, Harrison plate, and President's dining room
copyright by the White House Historical Association. Photographs by National Geographic Society

Soups

THOMAS JEFFERSON PENNED SOME IDEAS on the preparation of soups in the back of his family cookbook. He called it "Observations on Soups" and it's still good advice. "Observations on Soups: Always observe to lay your meat in the bottom of the pan with a lump of fresh butter. Cut the herbs and roots small and lay them over the meat. Cover it close and put it over a slow fire. This will draw forth the flavors of the herbs, and in a much greater degree than to put on the water at first. When the gravy produced from the meat is beginning to dry, put in the water and when the soup is done, take it off. Let it cool and skim off the fat clear. Heat it again and dish it up. When you make white soups, put in cream when you take it off the fire."

Braising endive is the classical French preparation of the Belgian vegetable. Endive has appeared on White House menus since the 18th century, and it was sometimes served as a potato substitute when the Kennedys occupied the White House. This is a different, but interesting, endive dish.

CHEF'S SPECIAL SOUP

1½ pounds Belgian endive
4 tablespoons butter
½ pound fresh mushrooms
2 tablespoons flour
1 teaspoon salt
1 tablespoon sugar
½ cup lemon juice
3 quarts chicken stock

Wash endive thoroughly; cut off rough ends and slice crosswise in ½-inch pieces up the stalks. Melt butter in a large saucepan or soup kettle and saute endive until it turns light brown; the last 5 minutes, add mushrooms that have been washed, peeled, and sliced in fairly thick slices. Sprinkle flour, salt, and sugar over the endive-mushroom mixture and blend. Stir in lemon juice and chicken stock and bring quickly to boiling; cook 1 to 2 minutes. Simmer, covered, about 30 minutes. *About 4 quarts soup*

President Kennedy was a soup fancier and often was served this favorite dinner menu: Rib Steak garnished with watercress, Potatoes Suzette, Mimosa Salad, Lemon Ice garnished with fresh strawberries, Assorted Cookies, and Demitasse. And the starter for this dinner was generally

CONSOMME JULIENNE A LA KENNEDY

1 small leek
1 small stalk celery
2 small carrots, scraped
2 slices turnip
3 cabbage leaves
½ medium onion, thinly sliced
1 tablespoon butter or margarine
⅛ teaspoon salt
   Dash of ground pepper
½ teaspoon sugar
4 chicken bouillon cubes, dissolved in 1 quart boiling water
   Parsley, chopped

Cut leek, celery, carrots, turnip, cabbage leaves, and onion into very thin strips **(julienne)** about 2 inches long. Melt butter in a medium-sized saucepan over low heat. Add vegetables, salt, pepper, and sugar. Cover and cook about 5 minutes until vegetables are tender. Combine with chicken bouillon; simmer 5 minutes. Garnish with chopped parsley before serving. *About 1 quart soup*

President Eisenhower's recipe for beef-vegetable soup is that of a gourmet; but his instructions are so complete that a novice cook could attempt it as a main dish meal, and serve it to company with the assurance of success. The ex-president did say that the best time to make vegetable soup is a day or so after fried chicken has been served. Save the uncooked necks, ribs, and back for the soup. While not absolutely necessary, they do "add something." A gourmet touch he used in the late spring, was to add nasturtium stems, for a flavor surprise; but only when they're young, green, and tender.

President Eisenhower's
GOURMET VEGETABLE SOUP

1 beef soup bone, split
2 pounds stewing meat, beef, mutton or a mixture
Several uncooked chicken pieces (necks, backs, wings)
1 tablespoon salt
Black pepper
6 tablespoons barley
½ cup fresh peas or cut green beans
2 medium potatoes, cut in ½-inch dice
2 or 3 stalks celery, cut in ½-inch dice
1 large onion, sliced
3 large carrots, cut in ½-inch dice
1 turnip, cut in ½-inch dice
1 cup chopped raw cabbage
½ cup canned corn, drained
1 quart canned tomatoes, drained
2 tablespoons prepared gravy seasoning
½ teaspoon celery salt
½ teaspoon onion salt
¼ teaspoon garlic salt

Place bone and stew meat, early in the morning, in a big kettle. Heavy aluminum is best, but a good iron pot will do almost as well. Drop in the bony parts of the chicken you have saved. Cover with water, something on the order of 3 quarts. Add a tablespoon of salt, a bit of black pepper, and, if you like, a touch of garlic (1 small clove). If you don't like garlic, put in an onion. Boil, covered, slowly all day long. Continue boiling until the meat has literally dropped off the bone. If your stock boils down during the day, add enough water from time to time to keep the meat covered. When the whole thing has practically disintegrated, pour into another large kettle through a colander. Make sure that the marrow is out of the bones. Let this drain through the colander for quite awhile, as much juice will drain out of the meat. (Shake the colander well to help get out all the juice.) Save a few of the better pieces of meat.

Put the kettle containing the stock you now have in a very cool place, outdoors in winter or in the ice box; let it stand all night and the next day until you are ready to make your soup. You will find that a hard layer of fat has formed on top of the stock which can usually be lifted off, since the whole kettle full of stock has jelled. Some people like a little bit of the fat left on and other like their soup very rich and do not remove more than about half of the fat.

In a separate pan, slowly boil the barley. This should be cooked separately since it has a habit, in a soup kettle, of settling to the bottom and if your fire should happen to get too hot, it is likely to burn. One of the secrets of making good vegetable soup is not to overcook any of the vegetables. However, it is impossible to give you an exact measure of the vegetables you should put in because some people like their vegetable soup almost as thick as stew, others like it much thinner. Moreover, sometimes you can get exactly the vegetables you want; other times you have to substitute. Where you use canned vegetables, put them in only a few minutes before taking the soup off the fire. If you use fresh ones, naturally they must be fully cooked in the soup. Add your vegetables, but they should not all be dumped in at once. The potatoes, for example, will cook more quickly than the carrots. Your effort must be to have them all nicely cooked but not mushy, at about the same time. The fire must not be too hot but the soup should keep bubbling. When you figure the soup is about done, put in your barley which should now be fully cooked, add 2 tablespoons of prepared gravy seasoning, and taste for flavoring particularly salt and pepper, and if you have it, use some onion salt, garlic salt, and celery salt. If you cannot get the gravy seasoning, use 2 teaspoons of Worcestershire sauce. Cut up the meat you have saved and put about a small handful into the soup. While you are cooking the soup do not allow the liquid to boil down too much. Add a bit of water from time to time. If your stock was thick when you started, you can add more water than if it was thin. As a final touch, in the springtime when nasturtiums are green and tender, you can take a few nasturtium stems, cut them up in small pieces, boil them separately as you did the barley, and add them to your soup, about 1 tablespoonful after cooking. *About 4 quarts soup*

George Washington was born in Westmoreland Co., Virginia, on Feb. 22, 1732. After his father, a land-owning planter, died in 1743, young Washington lived with relatives and received about eight years of schooling.

G. Washington

1ST PRESIDENT

1789-1797

Washington was sworn in as President in New York City in the spring of 1789 and served for two terms as the country's leader, guiding the new nation with firmness and imagination.

. . . a favorite of Teddy Roosevelt and a hearty, tasty winter meal.

BLACK BEAN SOUP

- 1 pound black beans
- 2 quarts water
- 1¼ tablespoons salt
- 1 cup diced carrot
- ½ cup diced celery
- ½ cup diced onion
- ¼ cup melted butter
- 1 ham bone or ¼ pound salt pork
  Dash cayenne pepper
- 1 tablespoon lemon juice
- 1 cup milk
- ¼ cup sherry (optional)

Soak beans overnight in water to cover. Drain beans and put in a large, covered kettle with the water. Add salt, bring to boiling, and skim top, if necessary. Reduce heat to simmer. Put carrot, celery, and onion in a skillet with butter and cook until golden. Add vegetables, ham bone, cayenne, and lemon juice to beans. Bring to boiling; quickly reduce heat to simmer. Cover and cook slowly until beans are done. Remove ham bone or salt pork; reserve pork. Drain the beans and vegetables, reserving the bean liquid. Force beans and vegetables through a sieve. Return sieved beans to a clean pot and add enough of the liquid, with 1 cup of milk, to make the soup the desired thickness. Reheat. If soup is too thick, thin with additional milk. Just before serving, mix in the sherry. Serve topped with croutons or diced salt pork. *About 2 quarts soup*

Since 1904 when House Speaker "Uncle Joe" Cannon thundered, "From now on, hot or cold, rain, snow or shine, I want it on the menu every day!" the popularity of Bean Soup has spread throughout Washington, D. C. . . . from Capitol Hill to this White House version.

SENATE BEAN SOUP

- 1 pound navy (pea) beans
- 3 quarts water
- 1 meaty ham bone
- 3 small onions, finely chopped
- 3 stalks celery, finely chopped
- 1 cup mashed potatoes
- 2 cloves garlic, minced
- ¼ cup chopped parsley

Soak beans in water overnight; drain. Pour 3 quarts water into a soup kettle. Add drained beans and the ham bone. Bring to boiling, skim, then cover and reduce heat to simmer. Cook, stirring occasionally, for about 1 hour. Add the remaining ingredients and continue simmering another hour. Remove ham bone and cut the meat into chunks. Return meat to soup and serve hot. *About 2 quarts soup*

Pièce de résistance of White House chefs, favorite of many Presidents, it is believed that Onion Soup was originated by a king. Returning late at night to his hunting lodge, Louis XV of France found only onions, butter, and champagne. Hungry and weary, he simply cooked them together and ... voila!

FRENCH ONION SOUP

16 to 18 medium onions
½ pound butter
3 cloves garlic, minced
2 stalks celery, minced
1 tablespoon minced parsley
2 tablespoons flour
6 cups beef bouillon
6 cups boiling water
1 ham bone, cleaned of meat
2 bay leaves
1 teaspoon ground thyme
Salt and pepper
French bread
Butter
1 clove garlic, bruised
Parmesan or Gruyère cheese, grated

Slice onions on the bias; this eliminates the worry about breaking up onion rings when they are stirred. Using a large saucepot, saute onions in butter until they have become **very** browned, but not burned. During the last few minutes, add the garlic, celery, and parsley. Sprinkle in flour and blend. Meanwhile, have heating in a large soup kettle, the beef bouillon and water. Add the ham bone, herbs, salt and pepper; blend with browned vegetables. Bring to boiling and cook 1 to 2 minutes, stirring constantly. Reduce heat to simmer, cover, and cook an hour; skim top, if necessary. Trim crusts from several slices of French bread, cube, and saute until golden brown in butter heated with remaining garlic. Sprinkle generously with Parmesan or Gruyère cheese. Place cubes on a baking sheet and broil until cheese is brown and bubbly. To serve: place some croutons in bottom of soup bowl or tureen, pour over some soup; croutons will float upwards. Pour on remainder of soup; garnish with additional croutons. Serve with bowls of additional Parmesan cheese. *About 4 quarts soup*

The tomatoless fish chowder that Kennedy carried in thermos bottles along his long campaign trail has been well publicized. Not so well known, but equally a favorite of the late president was

tomato soup, even the canned variety. Here is the White House recipe.

John F. Kennedy's
ICED TOMATO SOUP

6 large, ripe tomatoes, coarsely chopped
1 onion, chopped
¼ cup water
½ teaspoon salt
Dash of ground pepper
2 tablespoons tomato paste
2 tablespoons flour
2 chicken bouillon cubes, dissolved in 2 cups of boiling water
1 cup heavy cream

Combine chopped tomatoes, onion, water, salt, and pepper in a saucepan; cook over moderate heat 5 minutes. Combine tomato paste with flour and add to tomatoes with the chicken bouillon. Stirring constantly, bring to boiling and cook 1 to 2 minutes. Force mixture through a fine sieve and chill several hours. Before serving, blend in cream. Season to taste with more salt, if necessary. Garnish each serving with a thin slice of peeled **tomato**. *1¾ quarts soup*

Mary Rattley was family cook for the Hoovers and famous for her delicious meals. She served this tasty mushroom soup hot and garnished it with whipped cream. But it is equally delicious as a summer soup, served icy cold and garnished with a dab of sour cream.

MARY RATTLEY'S MUSHROOM SOUP

1 pound fresh mushrooms, finely chopped
1 pint cold water
1 pint chicken stock, seasoned
1 pint thin cream
1 tablespoon flour
Salt to taste
1 tablespoon milk
½ cup whipped cream

Add the cold water to the mushrooms and let stand 2 hours; cook about 30 minutes over low heat. Strain the mushroom liquid and chicken stock into a saucepan. Stir in all but ½ cup cream. Bring to boiling, stirring constantly. Meanwhile, blend flour, salt, milk and remaining ½ cup cream until smooth. Stir into the boiling soup and cook 1 to 2 minutes. Just before serving add whipped cream. 1 tablespoon per soup bowl. *About 1½ quarts soup*

Cream of watercress soup was a turn-of-the-century favorite almost overlooked today. It takes no special culinary skill to make and is delicious served hot or cold.

CREAM OF WATERCRESS SOUP

  3 tablespoons butter
½ cup chopped onion
  3 cups chopped watercress
  3 chicken bouillon cubes
¼ teaspoon dry mustard
  3 cups boiling water
  1 tablespoon flour
  2 cups milk
    Salt to taste
¼ teaspoon ground white pepper (optional)
  1 egg yolk
½ cup light cream

Smother the onion in butter and cook until soft but not browned. Add the watercress, cover, and gently cook another 3 minutes. Dissolve chicken bouillon cubes and dry mustard in boiling water. Blend flour into onion-watercress mixture. Add milk gradually, stirring constantly. Bring to boiling; cook 1 to 2 minutes. Slowly add bouillon and simmer for 15 to 20 minutes, stirring occasionally. Put mixture into an electric blender and puree at high speed. If you do not have a blender, then force mixture through a very fine sieve. Season to taste with salt and pepper; reheat. Beat egg yolk with cream; mix in a little of the hot soup. Add slowly to hot mixture, stirring constantly. This soup can be served hot, topped with a garnish of seasoned whipped cream; it can be served iced, garnished with sour cream sprinkled with paprika or a dash of liquid pepper seasoning. Other greens that adapt themselves to soup preparation are spinach, parsley, and romaine lettuce. *About 1½ quarts soup*

Popularly regarded as a French soup, Vichyssoise was developed in the United States by a French chef . . . to delight American tastes. This recipe was perfected in the White House kitchens.

VICHYSSOISE

  4 leeks, sliced paper thin
  1 medium onion, sliced paper thin
  6 tablespoons butter
  4 large red potatoes, cooked, peeled
    and sliced
  4 cups chicken stock
  2 cups milk
  2 cups cream
¼ teaspoon ground nutmeg
½ teaspoon salt
⅛ teaspoon ground pepper
  1 cup dairy sour cream
    Chopped chives

In a large saucepan cook the leeks and onion in the butter until soft, but not brown. Add potatoes and chicken stock. (Chicken stock is easily made by dissolving 4 chicken bouillon cubes and a pinch of dry mustard in 1 quart boiling water.) Cover and simmer 30 to 40 minutes. Cool and sieve or puree in the electric blender until smooth. Return soup to the heat, stir in the milk, cream, nutmeg, salt, and pepper. Bring slowly to boiling. Cool and sieve or blend until smooth a second time. Stir in sour cream and chill thoroughly. Sprinkle each portion with chopped chives. *About 2½ quarts soup*

2ND PRESIDENT
1797-1801

John Adams, born in Quincy (then part of Braintree), Mass., on Oct. 30, 1735, was the son of John Adams, a farmer and the village cobbler. Young John was graduated from Harvard College at 19 and then studied law.

John Adams was the first President to take up residence in the White House, which was opened in 1800.

CRAB BISQUE

2 tablespoons butter
1 tablespoon flour
2 hard-cooked eggs, sieved
  Grated peel of 1 lemon
1 teaspoon Worcestershire sauce
1 quart milk
½ cup heavy cream
1 teaspoon onion juice
  Pinch of ground mace
  Salt and pepper to taste
2 cups cooked, fresh crab meat or frozen
  Alaska king crab
½ cup sliced fresh mushrooms
½ cup sliced celery
1 tablespoon butter
¼ cup sherry

Blend melted butter, flour, sieved eggs, lemon peel and Worcestershire sauce to a paste and put into the top of a double boiler. Combine and scald milk and cream; blend in onion juice and mace. Adding slowly stir into paste in double boiler; bring to boiling over direct heat, stirring constantly. Cook 1 to 2 minutes. Set over simmering water. Add salt, pepper, and crab meat. Saute mushrooms and celery in the butter and add to bisque. Before serving, stir in the sherry.

About 1½ quarts soup

Here is the well-known Kennedy fish chowder made the traditional way, as you would expect it to be made for a Bostonian. It has been well publicized as the late president's favorite soup.

President Kennedy's
NEW ENGLAND FISH CHOWDER

2 pounds haddock
2 ounces salt pork, diced
2 onions, sliced
4 large potatoes, pared and diced
1 cup chopped celery
1 bay leaf, crumbled
1 teaspoon salt
  Freshly ground black pepper
1 quart milk
2 tablespoons butter

Place haddock with 2 cups water in a large saucepot; bring to boiling. Reduce heat and simmer 14 minutes, or until fish flakes easily with a fork. Drain and reserve broth. Remove bones from fish. Saute diced salt pork until crisp in the saucepot; remove and set aside. Saute onion in fat remaining in pot. Add fish, potatoes, celery, bay leaf, salt, and pepper. Pour in the fish broth with enough boiling water to make 3 cups liquid. Slowly bring to boiling; reduce heat and simmer, uncovered, 30 minutes. Add the milk and butter; simmer about 5 minutes, or until thoroughly heated. Serve chowder sprinkled with crisp salt pork.

About 3 quarts chowder

Oysters were one of the favorite foods in colonial America. They were so popular that vendors used to hawk them on the streets. When rudimentary refrigeration allowed railroads to carry them, oysters went west. While the Lincolns lived in Springfield, Illinois, they had oysters shipped from St. Louis for their "oyster suppers." Benjamin Harrison was another president who loved oysters in any form, and they were frequently found on his White House menus. Harrison's steward, Hugo Ziemann, used oysters in a sauce poured over steak! Rutherford B. Hayes wanted his oysters served as oyster stew (one of his great favorites) and still one of the popular ways of enjoying them.

Rutherford B. Hayes'
OYSTER STEW

¼ pound butter
½ cup chicken stock
½ teaspoon salt
  White pepper (optional)
1 teaspoon celery salt
  Pinch of paprika
1 tablespoon Worcestershire sauce
1 quart of fresh oysters
1 quart milk
2 cups heavy cream
4 tablespoons butter

Melt butter in a saucepan and add chicken stock, salt, pepper, celery salt, paprika, and Worcestershire sauce. When butter is hot and bubbly, add the oysters and their oyster liquor. Simmer the oysters gently in this liquor for 2 or 3 minutes or until their edges begin to curl. Meanwhile, scald milk and cream together and add the oyster mixture. Reheat, but do not boil. Serve piping hot in soup bowls, with a lump of butter floated in each bowl, and a bowl of **oyster crackers.**

About 1½ quarts soup

Although three presidents have been married while in office, only the wedding of Grover Cleveland to Frances Folsom was held in the White House. The ceremony took place in the Blue Room on June 2, 1882.

RED SNAPPER SOUP

1½- to 2-pound red snapper

White Wine Court Bouillon

    Fish trimmings (head, bones)
1 quart water
1 cup dry white wine
1 medium onion, quartered
1 medium carrot, sliced
2 slices lemon
3 whole cloves
3 whole peppercorns
    Celery tops
1 sprig parsley
1 bay leaf
1 teaspoon salt
    Pinch celery seed
    Pinch ground thyme
    Pinch ground marjoram

Remove fish head, skin, bones, fins, and tail from red snapper. Combine all other ingredients of the court bouillon except fish trimmings and bring quickly to boiling; add fish trimmings, cover, and reduce heat. Simmer 30 minutes, then strain stock. While stock is simmering, prepare brown sauce.

Special Brown Sauce

¼ cup flour
¼ cup butter
1 pint of chicken stock
2 cans (6 ounces each) tomato paste

Brown the flour in the butter. Adding gradually, stir in the chicken stock and tomato paste. Simmer slowly, stirring occasionally, while fish stock is cooking.

Now to complete the Red Snapper Soup:

¼ cup diced onion
¼ cup diced celery
½ cup diced green pepper
3 tablespoons butter
2 cups diced red snapper
¼ cup dry sherry

Saute onion, celery, and green pepper in butter until soft; blend in fish stock and bring to boiling. Slowly add the brown sauce, blending thoroughly, then bring to boiling again and cook 1 to 2 minutes. Add red snapper meat, and simmer until the fish is tender, 10 to 15 minutes. Before serving, stir in the sherry and serve hot.

About 2 quarts soup

11

Thomas Jefferson designed his home, *Monticello,* and built it on top of a "little mountain" overlooking the Virginia countryside. After his retirement this stately home became a mecca for distinguished guests from Europe and America.

President James K. Polk, too, was introduced to such gourmet dishes as Crayfish Bisque when he visited fascinating New Orleans after he left office in 1849.

President Jackson's
CRAYFISH BISQUE

- 2 fresh-frozen crayfish or rock-lobster tails, cooked according to package directions
- 1 medium onion, finely chopped
- 1 medium carrot, finely chopped
- ¼ cup butter
- ¼ cup flour
- 1 teaspoon salt
- ⅛ teaspoon pepper
- 5 cups quick chicken broth (5 chicken bouillon cubes dissolved in 5 cups boiling water)
- Few drops Tabasco
- 1 bay leaf
- 2 egg yolks, slightly beaten
- 1 cup cream

Remove crayfish meat from shells, chop very fine and reserve. Prepare vegetables and reserve. Heat butter in a kettle and stir in a mixture of flour, salt, and pepper. Heat until bubbly, then gradually blend in the broth with Tabasco, chopped vegetables, and bay leaf. Simmer, covered, 10 minutes, stirring occasionally. Add crayfish meat. Cover and simmer 10 minutes. Remove bay leaf and pour the hot mixture through a food mill, forcing through as much crayfish as possible. Return soup to kettle and reheat. Stir a small amount into egg yolks and return to kettle. Blend thoroughly. Cook and stir until well heated but do not boil. Stir in the cream and fish pieces remaining in food mill. Heat again and serve immediately.

About 1½ quarts soup

RHODE ISLAND CLAM CHOWDER

- 1 quart quahogs (hard-shell clams)
- 2-inch cube salt pork, finely diced
- 2 medium onions, sliced very thin
- 4 potatoes, pared and cut in ¾-inch cubes (4 cups)
- Salt and pepper to taste
- Flour
- 2½ cups hot chicken broth
- 4 cups milk, scalded
- 4 tablespoons butter
- 6 large pilot crackers

Wash and scrub clams in the shells, changing the water several times. Put into a kettle with 1 cup water. Cover tightly and steam until the shells open wide, about 30 minutes. Let stand a few minutes to allow sand to settle, then strain the liquid (broth) carefully and reserve. Chop finely the hard part (called "the foot") of the clams. Fry the salt pork slowly until crisp and brown; remove from the fat and reserve. Fry the onion in the pork fat about 5 minutes (do not brown) and turn into a stew pan. Parboil the potatoes 5 minutes in boiling water to cover; drain. Put a layer of potatoes in pan over onions; add the chopped part of clams. Sprinkle with salt, pepper, and flour. Add remaining potatoes; again add seasonings and flour. Add the chicken broth and cook 10 minutes. Add hot milk, soft part of clams and 3 tablespoons of the butter. Bring to boiling and cook about 3 minutes. Add crackers that have been split and soaked in enough cold milk to moisten them. Thicken the reserved clam broth with 1 tablespoon flour blended with 1 tablespoon butter. Stir the thickened broth into chowder just before serving. (Adding clam broth earlier will cause milk to separate.) Garnish servings of chowder with crisp salt pork.

About 2½ quarts chowder

Breads

HOT BREADS ARE AS AMERICAN as turkey with cranberry sauce, succotash, apple pie, or strawberry shortcake. One early traveler to America wrote of his distaste for American hot breads; he was certain the good ladies of America would all lose their teeth through the eating of them. Why, it was as bad as the American custom of putting milk into coffee! Today the bread basket, filled with fresh-from-the-oven morsels, continues to be a popular feature of American menus. Hot breads such as Sally Lunn, Johnny cake, hush puppies, muffins, cracknels, spoon bread, and many others are prepared from handed-down recipes originating in colonial kitchens. Here are some of those recipes adapted from the White House versions.

Mrs. Lyndon B. Johnson's
POPOVERS

1 cup sifted all-purpose flour
¼ teaspoon salt
2 eggs, beaten
1 cup milk
2 tablespoons shortening, melted

Mix and sift flour and salt into a bowl. Combine the last 3 ingredients and blend well. Gradually add to the dry ingredients beating constantly about 1 minute, or until batter is smooth. Fill greased sizzling-hot pans ¾ full and bake at 450°F. 20 minutes. Reduce heat to 350°F. and continue baking 15 to 20 minutes, or until deep golden brown.   *8 medium popovers*

Pat Nixon's
YORKSHIRE PUDDING

Pan drippings from roast beef
2 eggs, well beaten
1 cup milk
½ teaspoon salt
1 cup sifted all-purpose flour

After removing roast from pan, drain off most of the fat. Increase oven temperature to 425°F. and return pan to oven while quickly preparing the batter. Blend beaten eggs with milk and salt; add flour and beat until smooth. Immediately pour over hot drippings and bake 35 to 40 minutes. Serve the Yorkshire Pudding with roast beef.   *About 6 servings*

The settlers of Jamestown in 1608 watched in amazement as the Indians ground corn and made bread, which makes cornbread one of the earliest American foods. Some Southerners prefer white rather than yellow corn meal. The favorite bread of Andrew Jackson at his Tennessee home, the Hermitage, was old-fashioned southern-type spoon bread. Here is the recipe from the Hermitage kitchen, modified for clarification. The modern-day ingredients of flour, baking powder, and sugar are omitted—as most Southerners say they should be! Whether you use grits or corn meal, save any left-over spoon bread. Slice and fry in butter the next morning for a real taste treat.

Andrew Jackson's
SPOON BREAD

1 cup white hominy grits or water-ground
     white corn meal
1½ teaspoons salt
1 cup cold water
2 cups hot milk
2 eggs, beaten
3 tablespoons butter or margarine

Blend hominy grits with the salt and cold water in a heavy saucepan. Stir until smooth, then blend in the hot milk. Cook and stir over low heat until mixture begins to thicken. Remove from heat; add the eggs and the butter. Beat until well blended. Turn into a well-greased 1-quart casserole. Bake at 350°F. 45 minutes, or until firm to the touch. Serve with a spoon, hot from the casserole, and don't forget plenty of **butter!**   *About 6 servings*

BEATEN BISCUITS

4 cups sifted all-purpose flour
1 teaspoon sugar
1 teaspoon salt
½ cup lard or other shortening
1 cup milk

Blend the first 3 ingredients thoroughly. Using a pastry blender or 2 knives, cut in the lard until particles are the size of rice kernels. Add the milk and stir to make a stiff dough. Turn onto a lightly floured surface and knead until smooth, about 3 minutes. Then beat vigorously with a wooden mallet, turning occasionally to beat dough on reverse side. Beat about 30 minutes, or until dough blisters and has a satiny surface. Roll about ½ inch thick and cut with a floured 1½-inch round cutter. Transfer to baking sheets; prick biscuits uniformly, using a small pointed skewer. Bake at 350°F. 30 minutes, or until very delicately browned.

About 4 dozen 1½-inch biscuits

NOTE: For smaller biscuits, use a 1-inch round cutter.

The amusing title of this recipe, found in Mrs. Roosevelt's favorite cookbook, might have been applied as well to the children she raised in the White House. Add these hot buttered biscuits to your file of Christmas goodies.

FAT RASCALS

4 cups sifted all-purpose flour
¼ cup sugar
1 teaspoon salt
4 teaspoons baking powder
1½ cups butter or margarine
1 pound dried currants
1 cup milk (about)

Sift the first 4 ingredients together into a mixing bowl. Cut in the butter with a pastry blender or 2 knives until particles are the size of rice kernels. Stir in the currants. (If currants are too dry, pour boiling water over them in a strainer; spread out on absorbent paper to drain thoroughly.) Add the milk gradually, mixing with a fork until a soft dough forms. Shape lightly into a ball and roll out ½ inch thick on a lightly floured surface. Using a 2-inch cutter, cut dough into rounds. Place on ungreased baking sheets and bake at 450°F. 12 to 15 minutes, or until lightly browned. Split and butter the biscuits; serve hot. *About 3 dozen biscuits*

Johnny cakes were originally called "journey" cakes. They were tasty, flat enough to go into a saddlebag, and held up well during a long journey. This modern version of Johnny cake is lighter in texture than the so-called journey cakes.

JOHNNY CAKE

1 cup sifted all-purpose flour
¼ cup sugar
1 teaspoon baking powder
¾ teaspoon salt
½ teaspoon baking soda
1 cup yellow cornmeal
1 egg, well beaten
1 cup buttermilk or sour milk (see page 86)
2 tablespoons butter or margarine, melted
2 tablespoons molasses

Sift the first 5 ingredients together into a bowl; mix in the cornmeal. Make a well in center. Add a mixture of the last 4 ingredients (all at one time) to dry ingredients and beat with electric or rotary beater until just smooth (do not overbeat). Turn batter into a greased 8-inch square pan and spread to corners. Bake at 425°F. about 20 minutes, or until bread shrinks from side of pan and is lightly browned on top. Serve bread hot, broken or cut in squares, with **butter** or warm **maple syrup**.

One 8-inch square johnny cake

Calvin Coolidge's
CORN MUFFINS

1 cup yellow cornmeal
1 cup sifted all-purpose flour
2 tablespoons sugar
1 tablespoon baking powder
½ teaspoon salt
1 egg, well beaten
1 cup milk
¼ cup butter, melted

Mix dry ingredients. Add egg, milk, and butter which have been well blended. Beat batter until just smooth (do not overbeat). Spoon into well-greased muffin pans and bake at 425°F. about 25 minutes. *1 dozen muffins*

Gingerbread is one of our oldest known recipes; the Romans were making it 2,000 years ago. This is Martha Washington's old recipe and is quite rich and cake-like. The recipe calls for brandy but fruit juices or coffee can be substituted. It really needs no icing or sauce, but can be served with a vanilla sauce, or even a hot rum sauce.

Martha Washington's
SPICED GYNGERBREDE

2¾ cups sifted all-purpose flour
1 teaspoon baking soda
½ teaspoon salt
2 teaspoons ground ginger
1 teaspoon ground cinnamon
1 teaspoon ground mace
1 teaspoon ground nutmeg
½ cup hydrogenated shortening
2 tablespoons grated orange peel
½ cup packed brown sugar
3 eggs
¼ cup strained orange juice
¼ cup brandy
1 cup molasses

Sift the first 7 ingredients together and set aside. Cream shortening, orange peel, and brown sugar until thoroughly blended. Add eggs, one at a time, beating until light and fluffy after each addition. Heat orange juice and brandy until warm; add to molasses and mix well. Alternately add dry ingredients and molasses mixture to creamed mixture, beginning and ending with dry ingredients. Beat only until blended after each addition. Turn batter into a greased 9 x 9 x 2-inch baking pan. Bake at 350°F. 30 to 40 minutes, or until a cake tester inserted in center comes out clean. Cool in pan on cooling rack.

One 9-inch square gingerbread

STEAMED BOSTON BROWN BREAD

1 cup rye flour
1 cup whole wheat flour
1 cup yellow cornmeal
1½ teaspoons baking powder
1 teaspoon salt
¾ teaspoon baking soda
2 cups buttermilk or sour milk (see note page 86)
¾ cup molasses
1 cup dark seedless raisins

Mix the first 6 ingredients in a large bowl. Make a well in center and add, all at one time, a mixture of the buttermilk and molasses. Add the raisins and stir only enough to moisten the flour. Pour an equal amount of batter into 3 well-greased cans (18 to 20 ounces each). Fill not more than ⅔ full. Cover cans tightly with aluminum foil or baking parchment made secure with string. Place cans on a trivet or rack in bottom of a large kettle or steamer. Add boiling water to no more than one half the height of the cans. Cover tightly and bring water to boiling. Reduce heat but keep water boiling gently. Steam bread 3 hours, adding more water if needed. Remove cans from kettle; run a knife around inside of cans to loosen loaves and unmold onto cooling rack. Serve warm, or store the cooled loaves (wrapped in moisture-vaporproof material) in a cool place. Reheat to serve.

3 loaves (about 1 pound each)

This is a basic light roll mixture, easy to make . . . but remember to start a day ahead of time! Use this dough for Parker House rolls, pan rolls, crescent rolls, pecan buns, or coffee cake.

BASIC LIGHT YEAST-ROLL DOUGH

¾ cup butter, softened
1 cup boiling water
2 teaspoons salt
½ cup sugar
2 packages active dry yeast
½ cup warm water (105°-115°F.)
2 eggs, beaten
¾ cup ice water
6½ to 7½ cups all-purpose flour

Mix the first 4 ingredients in a large bowl until well blended; cool. Soften yeast in warm water in a bowl. Stir a blend of yeast, eggs and ice water into first mixture. Add about 3 cups flour, ½ cup at a time, beating vigorously after each addition until batter is smooth. Mix in enough remaining flour to make a soft dough that does not stick to sides of bowl. Turn onto a lightly floured surface, let rest 5 to 10 minutes, then knead until satiny and smooth. Form into a ball and place in greased bowl. Turn dough to bring greased surface to top. Cover tightly and refrigerate overnight. Remove dough and punch down. Brush top with oil, cover, and let rise in a warm place until doubled. (This can take from 1 to 2½ hours.) Shape as desired. If shaped into rolls, place rolls on greased baking sheets and let rise in a warm place until light. Bake at 425°-450°F. 12 to 18 minutes, depending on size of rolls.

5 to 6 dozen rolls

President Johnson's
FAVORITE BANANA BREAD

½ cup butter
1 cup sugar
2 eggs
3 ripe bananas, mashed (1 cup)
2 cups all-purpose flour
1 teaspoon baking soda
¼ teaspoon salt
1 cup buttermilk or sour milk (see note page 86)

Cream butter until softened; beat in the sugar until thoroughly blended. Add the eggs, one at a time, beating until fluffy after each addition. Beat in mashed banana. Blend dry ingredients and beat into creamed mixture alternately with buttermilk. Mix only until blended. Turn batter into a greased 9 x 5-inch loaf pan. Bake at 350°F. 50 to 60 minutes.   *One loaf banana bread*

Although this is a modern recipe using some prepared ingredients it is a delicious addition to any barbecue menu.

BARBECUE QUICK BREAD

2 teaspoons garlic salad dressing mix
¼ cup shredded Parmesan cheese
2 cups biscuit mix
1 tablespoon sugar
1 egg, well beaten
½ cup milk
¼ cup butter or margarine, melted
¼ cup dry white wine

Combine the first 4 ingredients in a mixing bowl; mix well. Blend in a mixture of the egg, milk, and butter and the wine. Mix only until dry ingredients are moistened. Turn into a well-greased 8-inch round cake pan (or pie pan). Bake at 400°F. 25 to 30 minutes. Serve warm cut in wedge-shaped pieces.   *About 6 servings*

For those who prefer rolls with more "body" than those made from the basic light yeast-roll dough, the potato roll has long been an American favorite. Martha Washington and Dolly Madison both had good potato roll recipes and they thought nothing of preparing rolls to serve to 50 people at dinner. Both recipes would be extremely arduous to prepare today. Dolly's starts out with this advice: "Boil 3 pounds potatoes, bruise and work them with 2 ounces butter, and as much milk as will make them pass through a colander. Take half or three-quarters of a pint of yeast . . ." et cetera. Using basically the same ingredients as Dolly Madison did, here is a modernized "receipt" for potato rolls.

POTATO ROLLS

2 packages active dry yeast
½ cup warm water (105°-115°F.)
1 cup milk, scalded
½ cup sugar
1½ teaspoons salt
1 cup mashed potato
⅔ cup hydrogenated shortening
2 eggs, well beaten
5 to 6 cups all-purpose flour

Soften the yeast in warm water. Combine the milk and next 4 ingredients in a large mixing bowl; beat until thoroughly blended. When lukewarm stir in the softened yeast. Beat in the eggs. Add about 3 cups flour, ½ cup at a time, beating vigorously after each addition. Mix in enough remaining flour to make a soft (but not sticky) dough. Turn onto a lightly floured surface, let rest 5 to 10 minutes, and knead until satiny and smooth. Form dough into a ball and put into a greased bowl. Turn to bring greased surface to top. Cover and refrigerate until thoroughly chilled. Remove dough and form into plain rolls or other desired shape. Place on greased baking sheets; cover and let rise in a warm place until doubled, about 45 minutes. Bake at 425°F. 12 to 15 minutes. Remove from oven and brush rolls lightly with melted **butter**.   *3 to 3½ dozen rolls*

Thomas Jefferson was born in Goochland (now Albemarle) Co., Virginia, Apr. 13, 1743. Privately tutored, he entered the College of William and Mary in 1760 to study law. He began, in 1769, to build his house Monticello and brought his bride there in 1772.

3RD PRESIDENT 1801-1809

Th. Jefferson

The yield of the basic light yeast-roll dough recipe depends on the size and shape desired, but the yield is large. Unless you are a very experienced cook, do not try to cut the recipe. Better to use some of the dough for this delicious special. . . .

HONEY PECAN TWIST

Basic Light Yeast-Roll Dough (page 15)
Topping
   ¼ cup butter or margarine, softened
   ⅔ cup packed brown sugar
   2 tablespoons honey
   1 egg white, unbeaten
   ¼ cup chopped pecans

To prepare two 8-inch twists, divide the basic dough recipe in half after the first rising. Set aside one portion to shape into rolls. Turn remaining portion onto lightly floured surface. Let rest 5 to 10 minutes, then divide in half. Shape each half into a long "rope" 1 inch in diameter. (For easier handling, again divide the dough for each twist equally before rolling, forming 2 "ropes" 1 inch in diameter for each pan.) Starting at the outside of a greased 8-inch round cake pan (or pie pan), wind the dough in a spiral toward center of pan. Join a second "rope" to first and continue spiraling, covering bottom of pan. Form a spiral in second pan using remaining dough. Set aside while preparing topping. Cream the butter with sugar, honey, and egg white, beating until fluffy. Blend in the nuts. Spread half of the mixture evenly over each twist. Cover lightly and let rise in a warm place until very light. Bake at 375°F. 25 to 30 minutes.

Two 8-inch coffee cakes

This hot-bread delicacy, of English origin, is sometimes baked in individual loaves or deep muffin-pan wells. In colonial days it was usually baked in a Turk's-head mold or other round mold. Sliced and toasted, the bread was an afternoon-tea favorite.

SALLY LUNN I

   ¾ cup milk, scalded and cooled to warm
   1 package active dry yeast
   ¼ cup warm water (105°-115°F.)
   ½ cup butter
   ⅓ cup sugar
   3 eggs (about ¾ cup)
   3¾ cups all-purpose flour
   1¼ teaspoons salt

Soften the yeast in warm water. Cream the butter until softened; add sugar gradually, beating constantly until thoroughly blended. Add eggs, one at a time, beating until fluffy after each addition. Combine warm milk with softened yeast; mix well. Blend flour and salt; add to creamed mixture alternately with yeast-milk mixture, beating vigorously after each addition. Scrape down dough from sides of bowl. Cover with waxed paper and a towel and let rise in a warm place until doubled, 1 to 1½ hours. When dough has doubled, beat thoroughly with a wooden spoon. Then turn into a well-greased 9- or 10-inch tubed pan or Turk's-head mold. Cover and let rise in a warm place until very light. Bake at 350°F. 40 to 45 minutes, or until golden brown on top.

One 9-inch round loaf

If you are planning a light luncheon or supper, a good, substantial bread can assume importance. Here is a hearty but light-textured, old-fashioned bread, just made for a soup, salad, or soufflé accompaniment.

OLD-FASHIONED HERB BREAD

   1 package active dry yeast
   ¼ cup warm water (105°-115°F.)
   ¾ cup milk, scalded
   3 tablespoons shortening
   3 tablespoons sugar
   1½ teaspoons salt
   3 to 3½ cups all-purpose flour
   1 egg, beaten
   ¼ teaspoon ground nutmeg
   2 teaspoons crushed sage

Soften yeast in warm water. Combine milk, shortening, sugar, and salt in a large mixing bowl. Blend well and cool to lukewarm. Add 1 cup flour and beat thoroughly. Beat in the egg, nutmeg, and sage, then the softened yeast. Mix in enough remaining flour to make a soft (but not sticky) dough. Turn onto a floured surface and knead until smooth and elastic. Place in a greased bowl; turn to bring greased surface to top. Let rise in a warm place until doubled, about 1 hour. Punch down dough and let rest about 10 minutes. Then shape into a round loaf. Place in a greased 9-inch pie pan and let rise in warm place until doubled, about 45 minutes. For a glossy crust, brush lightly with slightly beaten **egg white**. Sprinkle top with 2 teaspoons **caraway seed**. Bake at 400°F. 10 minutes; reduce heat to 375°F. and bake 20 to 25 minutes longer.

One 9-inch round loaf bread

Here's a buttery-rich version of the delicious hot bread served often in colonial Williamsburg.

SALLY LUNN II

- 1 package active dry yeast
- ¼ cup warm water (105°-115°F.)
- ½ cup milk, scalded
- ⅔ cup butter, softened
- 2 tablespoons sugar
- ¾ teaspoon salt
- 2 cups sifted all-purpose flour
- 2 eggs, well beaten

Soften the yeast in warm water. Pour the hot milk over butter, sugar, and salt in a large mixing bowl. Blend well and when lukewarm add about ½ cup flour; beat until smooth. Stir the yeast and add to batter; mix well. Add about half of the remaining flour and beat until very smooth. Add eggs and beat until thoroughly blended. Beat in remaining flour and continue beating no less than 5 minutes. Scrape down the sides of bowl. Cover with waxed paper and a towel; let rise in a warm place until doubled, about 45 minutes. Then beat again about 5 minutes. Turn into a greased 1½-quart ring mold or Turk's-head mold. Cover and let rise until doubled, about 45 minutes. Bake at 350°F. 25 to 35 minutes, or until golden brown. Run a knife around edge of mold to loosen the ring; gently remove to cooling rack. Serve warm.   *One loaf*

TEXAS BRAN BREAD

- 1½ cups boiling water
- 3 tablespoons shortening
- 3 tablespoons brown sugar
- 2 tablespoons molasses
- 2 teaspoons salt
- 1 cup whole bran
- 1 package active dry yeast
- ½ cup warm water (105°-115°F.)
- 5 to 5½ cups all-purpose flour

Pour boiling water over the next 5 ingredients in a large bowl. Blend well and set aside to cool to lukewarm. Soften the yeast in warm water. Beat 1 cup flour into bran mixture. Stir softened yeast and beat into batter. Continue beating while gradually adding about half of remaining flour. Beat vigorously, then mix in enough remaining flour to make a soft (but not sticky) dough. Lightly grease top of dough. Cover and let rise in a warm place until doubled, about 2 hours. Turn onto a lightly floured surface and knead gently until smooth and "springy." Divide

in half and shape into 2 loaves. Put into 2 greased 8½ x 4½ x 2½-inch loaf pans. Cover and let rise until almost doubled, about 45 minutes. Bake at 325°F. (oven not preheated) 50 to 55 minutes. Remove loaves from oven and turn onto cooling rack. Lightly brush with melted **butter**.
2 loaves bread

A typical White House luncheon menu of 1933 (days of FDR) read like this: Clear bouillon, butter thin crackers, chicken a la king in patty shells, candied sweet potatoes, green beans, sweet pickles, brick ice cream, assorted cookies, and coffee. The breads might be cornbread or whole wheat bread which was a particular favorite of Mrs. FDR. Her recipes for breads generally made a coarser bread than is favored today, for that is the way Mrs. Roosevelt liked it. When she traveled in Europe, she always made a special point to enjoy some of the peasants' black bread, along with strong cheese.

Mrs. F. D. Roosevelt's
WHOLE WHEAT BREAD

- 3 cups unsifted whole wheat flour (stone ground)
- 2 tablespoons brown sugar
- 1 tablespoon salt
- ¾ cup molasses
- 2 tablespoons shortening, melted
- 3½ cups water
- 2 packages active dry yeast
- ½ cup warm water (105°-115°F.)
- 8 cups all-purpose flour (about)

Mix the first 6 ingredients in a large bowl. Soften yeast in warm water. Stir the yeast and add to flour-molasses mixture. Beat in 2 cups of the flour, ½ cup at a time, beating vigorously after each addition. Mix in enough remaining flour to make a soft (but not sticky) dough. Cover bowl with aluminum foil and refrigerate about 8 hours or overnight. Punch down dough and turn onto lightly floured surface; divide into thirds and shape into 3 loaves. Put into 3 greased loaf pans or pie pans (for round loaves). Cover and let rise in a warm place until light (but not doubled). Bake at 400°F. 15 minutes; reduce heat to 350°F. and bake 40 minutes, or until loaves are golden brown and sound hollow when tapped. Remove from pans onto cooling racks. Brush tops with melted **butter**.   *3 loaves bread*

Cheese Dishes

WHEN THE WHITE HOUSE WAS FIRST OCCUPIED in 1800, cheese had been on mankind's menu for thousands of years. If it is true that the Pilgrim Fathers had landed "with a cookbook under one arm and a Bible under the other," we have a clue to the source of the Colonial dames' familiarity with cheese and cheese recipes. Among the available foods of the time, cheese is frequently mentioned in American court records of the eighteenth century (in Washington's time).

Widely traveled, internationally known, almost infinitely varied, cheeses have been served at the White House in many such dishes as these:

President and Mrs. Kennedy opened the White House Fall social season in 1961 with a reception honoring the members of the Supreme Court. Champagne was served, and on the buffet table in the State Dining Room were such delicacies as hot and cold canapés, lobster, shrimp, cold turkey, mousse of foie gras, and a French classic, Quiche Lorraine. It's a cheese and onion pie to be served as a buffet, light luncheon, or supper dish. Accompany it with a Caesar salad, or your favorite mixed greens, and chilled dry white wine.

QUICHE LORRAINE

Pastry for 1-crust 10-inch pie (1½ times recipe, page 95)
6 slices bacon
¼ cup finely chopped onion
¼ cup grated Parmesan cheese
6 slices Swiss cheese
2 cups milk
3 whole eggs, slightly beaten
2 extra egg yolks
2 tablespoons flour
¼ teaspoon salt
2 tablespoons butter, melted

Prepare pastry; roll it ⅛ inch thick, and line a 10-inch pie pan. Flute or crimp the edge. Cut bacon slices into thin strips; fry slowly over low heat until crisp. Drain the bacon on absorbent paper. Saute the onion in bacon fat until tender. Drain onion and mix with the Parmesan cheese. Cut Swiss cheese slices into thin strips; arrange the cheese strips and bacon strips so that they overlap in the bottom of the pie pan. Sprinkle Parmesan-onion mixture over them. Combine milk, slightly beaten eggs, egg yolks, flour, and salt; mix thoroughly. Stir in melted butter. Pour mixture into pie pan. Bake at 375°F. about 40 minutes, or until a silver knife inserted near the center comes out clean. About 15 minutes before the pie is done, sprinkle lightly with **nutmeg** and return to oven. *6 servings*

NOTE: Although it is a traditional recipe, there can be many variations for those cooks who like to experiment with flavors. Try substituting smoked salmon, cooked crab meat or shrimp, or sauteed sliced mushrooms for the bacon.

Welsh rabbit is generally prepared in a chafing dish or double boiler, over simmering water. But the secret of Welsh Rabbit is gentle heat. You can make it in an electric fry pan on low heat instead of over water.

WELSH RABBIT

2 eggs
¼ teaspoon salt
¼ teaspoon paprika
½ teaspoon dry mustard
1 teaspoon Worcestershire sauce
2 tablespoons butter
1 pound sharp cheddar cheese, shredded
1 cup beer or ale

Beat eggs lightly, just enough to mix yolk and white. Add salt, paprika, dry mustard, and Worcestershire sauce to eggs and set aside. Melt butter at a low temperature in an electric fry pan and add the cheese. Stir until the cheese is melted. Stirring must be constant from this step until completion of the dish. Very slowly stir in the beer or ale. When blended, slowly stir in the egg mixture. (Whether you are using a double boiler or electric fry pan, do not let egg mixture overheat or eggs will curdle.) When mixture is thick and warmed through, spoon over slices of **toast.** *6 servings*

This easy Cheese Soufflé is likely to be a family favorite. It is prepared the day before baking.

EASY CHEESE SOUFFLE

2 jars (5 ounces each) pasteurized process sharp cheddar cheese spread
1 stick (¼ pound) butter
8 slices bread
4 eggs
2 cups milk

Let butter soften at room temperature; then blend it thoroughly with the cheese spread. Trim the crusts from the bread; spread the bread slices generously with the cheese-butter mixture. Then cut the bread into bite-size pieces. Grease a 1½- or 2-quart casserole and place the bread pieces in it. Beat eggs lightly and combine with milk. Pour egg-milk mixture over bread pieces. Refrigerate overnight. Bake at 350°F. 1 hour.

4 to 6 servings

NOTE: This easy Cheese Soufflé is enhanced by serving a mushroom or a shrimp sauce over it.

Thomas Jefferson is credited with the introduction of macaroni and other pastas to America. Another famous Democrat, the late John F. Kennedy, popularized fettucine, a Roman pasta not generally appreciated here until it became one of the late president's favorite dishes. When traveling in California, Kennedy always ordered fettucine "to go" from one of the famous restaurants on the coast. The special hard-wheat flour used by commercial pasta makers is not generally available to the public, but you can still make good fettucine dough at home. The secret to its melt-in-the-mouth goodness is to roll the noodle dough paper-thin.

FETTUCINE A LA KENNEDY

1 pound Fettucine Noodles (see recipe)
6 tablespoons unsalted butter
1 cup dairy sour cream
1 cup heavy cream
½ cup grated Parmesan cheese
2 tablespoons chopped chives
Salt, pepper, nutmeg to taste

Use plenty of boiling, salted water and cook noodles, drain, and set aside. Homemade fettucine noodles take less time (cook about 5 minutes) than do "store" noodles. In either case, cook noodles until just tender. Melt butter in a skillet and add noodles. Add sour cream and stir over very low heat. Add cream and cook slowly for 5 minutes. Stir in Parmesan cheese, 1 tablespoon chives, and salt, pepper and nutmeg; continue stirring until cheese is melted. Garnish with remaining chives.

4 servings

Fettucine Noodles

3½ cups sifted all-purpose flour
4 eggs
¼ teaspoon salt
1 tablespoon light cream

Put flour on a pastry board and make a well. Break eggs into the center. Add salt and cream. Mix and knead as you would bread dough, kneading with the heel of your hand and slapping dough down on the board as you work it. Knead until dough is very shiny, a minimum of 15 minutes, at least. Divide dough into 3 pieces, and shape into balls. Work each ball separately, rolling out on a floured surface. When dough is rolled out paper-thin, flour it very lightly, roll it up, and cut into ½-inch strips. Unroll strips and dry on towels 30 minutes.

1 pound noodles

The French "puff" their soufflés quickly in a very hot oven and the insides are likely to be a little "runny." If you want your soufflé light, but solid all the way through (as most Americans are accustomed to), add another 10 minutes baking time.

FRENCH CHEESE SOUFFLE

¼ cup butter
¼ cup flour
1½ cups milk, scalded
¼ cup shredded sharp cheddar cheese
1 teaspoon salt
6 eggs, separated
1 additional egg white

Melt butter, then blend in flour and cook until bubbly, stirring constantly. Add hot milk gradually, stirring until smoothly blended; bring to boiling and cook 1 to 2 minutes. Add the shredded cheese and salt and stir until smooth. Beat the egg yolks and stir into cheese sauce. Beat the egg whites, including the additional one, until stiff, not dry, peaks are formed. Egg white should be at room temperature. Fold the egg whites into the cheese mixture. If you don't have a soufflé dish, butter a 2-quart straight-sided casserole. Pour the mixture into the casserole and bake at 425°F. about 20 minutes, or until well puffed and lightly browned.

4 to 6 servings

"County Election" by artist-politician George Bingham, expresses the excitement and holiday atmosphere of election day in the turbulent times of James Buchanan's presidency.

Meats

. . . including barbequeing notes from George to Lyndon

WE DON'T KNOW OF ANY PRESIDENTS who didn't like steak! In Washington's time they broiled their steaks on a "gridiron" (griddle) over a "clear, brisk fire," and sent them to the tables garnished with finely chopped shallots.

Jefferson marinated his steaks in salted olive oil for 2 hours before broiling. Then they were served with a delicious maître d'hôtel butter. You cannot beat that kind of cooking today! Then there's the story of Abe Lincoln, a familiar sight in Springfield (Ill.) strolling back from the butcher with a brown package under his arm. This usually contained enough steak for a meal for the family and the price of the package was ten cents!

President Grant insisted that his beef be well-done. Teddy Roosevelt, the great outdoorsman, chefed his own food when on one of his many camping trips. He liked his steaks panfried in bacon grease over a campfire.

President Eisenhower, an amateur chef of some fame, especially enjoyed cooking for his grandchildren. In fact, you can call both Presidents Eisenhower and Kennedy "steak, baked potato, and tossed green salad men." Americans have the world's best beef and benefit from that fact in that most Americans favor a succulent steak, grilled simply on the barbeque or over hot coals in the fireplace. And most every man has his own idea about how to grill a steak. When chefing for friends, ask them to what degree of doneness they prefer their steak. If they say they don't care, press harder. You'll find they do care. The way to cook a good steak is by experience.

STEAK DIANE

- 2 tablespoons butter
- 1 clove garlic, bruised
- 2 pounds beef tenderloin, sliced ¼ inch thick
  Salt and pepper
- ½ teaspoon dry mustard
- ½ teaspoon fresh lemon juice
- ½ cup finely chopped green onion (with tops)
- 3 tablespoons sherry
- 1 tablespoon cognac

Melt butter, add bruised garlic and brown, then discard garlic. Salt and pepper, then pan-broil steaks in the garlic butter 2 minutes on each side. Remove steaks and keep warm. Stir in mustard, lemon juice, and onion, cooking onion until transparent but not brown. Add sherry and cognac. Heat 2 minutes, or it may be **flambéed** if made in a chafing dish, but do not boil (if flambéed, additional brandy may be required to flame). Pour over steaks and serve.   *4 servings*

Richard M. Nixon's

BRAISED SWISS STEAKS

- 2 tablespoons corn oil
- 1 large onion, sliced
- ¼ teaspoon thyme
- 6 8-ounce steaks (cut from top round)
- 1 cup cocktail vegetable juice
- 1 cup beef bouillon
- 1½ cups carrots, leeks, and celery, cut in julienne (thin strips)
- 1 teaspoon chopped parsley

Heat half of the oil in a skillet. Add onion and simmer until golden. Remove from heat and add thyme. Sprinkle the steaks on both sides with **seasoned salt,** then coat with **flour.** Heat remaining oil in a large skillet. Add steaks and brown on both sides. Transfer steaks to skillet with onion. Pour vegetable juice and bouillon over steaks. Cover skillet and cook 1 hour over low heat or in a 350°F. oven. After 1 hour of cooking, turn steaks over, cover with vegetables, and continue cooking 30 minutes. To serve, arrange steaks on serving platter. Spoon sauce and vegetables over steaks. Sprinkle with parsley.

6 servings

CHARCOAL GRILLED STEAK

- 1 sirloin steak, 1 to 1½ inches thick
  Salt and pepper
- ½ teaspoon of liquid barbeque smoke
  Charcoal

Start your charcoal fire 30 minutes ahead of time. When the charcoal is ash white, the fire is hot enough to grill the steak. Rub the steak with salt and pepper and brush meat on both sides with liquid barbeque smoke. Place the steak on the grill. In a few moments fat dropping in the charcoal will cause the charcoal to flame yellow. This is good. Let the flames sear the steak (turning once to get both sides) for a minute and seal in the juices. Then take a baster and squirt a little water on the charcoal. That will put out the flame and raise a nice smoke. Continue cooking, turning the steaks with tongs, occasionally, for 10 to 15 minutes, or until your desired degree of doneness is attained.   *About 4 servings*

ROAST STEAK BRIZZOLA

- 1 steak (porterhouse, sirloin, or New York strip) at least 1½ inches thick, 2 is better
- 1 clove garlic, cut
- 3 tablespoons olive oil
- 1 tablespoon Worcestershire sauce
- 2 tablespoons crumbled blue cheese
  Pinch of garlic powder
  Salt and pepper to taste
- 4 tablespoons butter

Rub steak well on both sides with ½ clove of fresh garlic. Discard garlic. Combine olive oil, Worcestershire sauce, blue cheese, garlic powder, and salt and pepper to make a thin flavoring paste. Melt butter in a large, shallow baking pan and when the butter foams, sear the steak on both sides in the butter. Remove from fire and spread flavoring paste over the top of the steak. Roast steak in a 400°F. oven. The time will vary anywhere from 20 minutes to 40 minutes. One cannot give a standard cooking time for rare or well-done meat. A meat thermometer can always be inserted. When steak is ready to serve, cut slices at a 45-degree angle across the grain and spoon pan juices over them.

About 4 servings

James Madison was born at Port Conway, Va., Mar. 16, 1751. He received his B. A. from the College of New Jersey, 1771. Upon his father's death, he inherited Montpelier, the family home, at the foot of the Blue Ridge Mountains in Virginia.

4TH PRESIDENT

1809-1817

As a delegate to the Continental Congress from 1780 to 1783, Madison took ample notes, which are now historically significant.

Dwight D. Eisenhower's

BEEF STEW FOR 60

20 pounds of stewing meat (round)
Cooking oil or shortening
3 gallons beef stock
Salt and pepper
Monosodium glutamate
8 pounds small Irish potatoes
6 bunches small carrots, scrubbed
5 pounds small onions
15 fresh tomatoes
1 bouquet garni (see below)
1½ cups shortening
3½ cups flour
½ cup cornstarch

Cube and brown beef in cooking oil and then stew meat until tender in beef stock, adding salt, pepper and monosodium glutamate. Add the vegetables, except tomatoes, and a bouquet garni (thyme, bay leaves, garlic, peppercorns, and whole cloves tied in a cheesecloth bag). Simmer, covered, until vegetables are done. Stir in tomatoes, cut in pieces, and heat thoroughly. Strain off 2 gallons of stock from the stew and thicken slightly with beef roux (Blend 1½ cups shortening either butter, shortening or a mixture of the two with 3½ cups flour and ½ cup cornstarch, then, gradually add some of the stock, stirring constantly until smooth; return to the remaining stock. — Editor.) Bring stew to boiling and slowly add stock, stirring constantly; boil about 5 minutes and simmer 30 minutes longer. Remove bouquet garni before serving.

Dwight D. Eisenhower's

BEEF STEW FOR 6

3 pounds prime round
½ cup cooking oil
2 cans beef bouillon
1 can water
Salt and pepper to taste
Monosodium glutamate
1 pound small Irish potatoes
½ bunch carrots (2 or 3 medium)
6 small onions
2 large tomatoes, peeled, chopped
1 bouquet garni (see below)
¼ cup butter
2 tablespoons flour
1 tablespoon cornstarch

Cut beef into 1½-inch cubes and brown in the cooking oil or shortening. Add bouillon, water, salt, pepper, monosodium glutamate, and simmer until meat is tender (pan covered). Add the vegetables, except tomatoes, and a bouquet garni (1 bay leaf, 1 whole clove, 2 peppercorns, pinch of thyme, and a bruised clove of garlic tied in a cheesecloth bag). Simmer again until vegetables are tender (about 30 minutes). Stir in tomatoes and heat thoroughly. Strain off 1 cup of liquid and thicken it with a beef roux (¼ cup butter, 2 tablespoons flour, and 1 tablespoon cornstarch blended as roux in recipe for Eisenhower's Beef Stew for 60). Bring stew to boiling and slowly add the stock, stirring constantly; boil 1 to 2 minutes and simmer 10 minutes longer. Remove bouquet garni before serving.

23

The early New England woman did not find life easy, and the New England Boiled Dinner was a result of expediency. At best, her home was often a log cabin of one or two rooms. The house was heated and the cooking done by, and in, the same open fireplace with an array of pots, pans, hooks, cranes, and big black kettles. While Mother was busy keeping her family warm, it was convenient for her to hang a big kettle over the warming fire and, from time to time, throw in such victuals as she might have to feed her family. And the New England Boiled Dinner was born.

NEW ENGLAND BOILED DINNER

2½-pound corned beef brisket
4 medium onions, peeled
4 medium carrots, pared
2 turnips, pared and cubed
1 medium cabbage, quartered
4 medium potatoes, pared and halved
4 medium beets
1 cup boiling water

Place meat in a large kettle; cover with cold water. Cover kettle; bring quickly to boiling and then reduce heat and simmer 2½ to 3 hours. About 45 minutes before the meat is finished, put in the onions, carrot, turnip, and pile the quartered cabbage on top. After 20 minutes, add potatoes and simmer another 20 minutes or so. The beets are really best cooked alone, covered in 1 cup boiling water, and simmered in a covered saucepan about 20 minutes, then peeled. Arrange meat on a platter and garnish with the vegetables.   *4 servings*

Ravigote means "revive" in French. And that's just what happens to this unusual brisket dish. It is prepared the day before serving, giving the flavors time to marry. Then it is "revived" and served the next day. Don't be afraid to try this recipe on guests. They'll be asking for your recipe!

FRESH BRISKET OF BEEF, RAVIGOTE

5-pound fresh beef brisket
½ cup seasoned flour
2 tablespoons cooking oil
1 bottle (8 ounces) creamy thick French
    dressing
½ cup home-style chili sauce
½ cup sherry
2 tablespoons chopped chives
2 tablespoons chopped parsley

Dredge brisket in flour, seasoned with salt and

pepper, and sear in cooking oil over high heat. Remove brisket to a 5-quart pottery casserole or a small, covered roasting pan. Pour French dressing over the meat, cover, and bake at 325°F. allowing 45 minutes per pound. About halfway through the cooking time add the chili sauce, sherry, chives, and parsley. When brisket is done, remove from oven and let cool. Refrigerate overnight in the pan it was cooked in with all the pan juices remaining. By morning the excess fat found in brisket will have risen to the top and solidified. Remove all the solid fat, and return to refrigerator. Reheat slowly in the pan juices, before slicing and serving.
About 8 servings

President Andrew Johnson was a reconstructionist president, but his culinary sympathies were strictly Dixie. His hostess was his daughter, Martha Patterson, and her recipes came from a small cookbook titled The Dixie Cookbook. It is still in the possession of her direct descendants. And a popular recipe, particularly in Johnson's home state of Tennessee, was, and is, Spiced Round of Beef. Now, for a modern-day version:

SPICED ROUND OF BEEF, TENNESSEE STYLE

Cooking oil
1 large onion, sliced
3-pound beef pot roast (round)
½ cup flour
Salt and pepper
2 cups water
½ cup cider vinegar
1 cup seedless raisins
¼ cup home-style chili sauce
3 whole cloves
2 bay leaves
10 gingersnaps

In a Dutch oven or a heavy, covered pan, heat some cooking oil, enough to cover the bottom of the pan; saute the onion until limp and glossy. While onion is cooking, cut the meat into 1½-inch cubes; dredge meat with flour, seasoned with salt and pepper. Push onion to side of pan and quickly brown meat on all sides. Add water, vinegar, raisins, chili sauce, cloves, and bay leaves. Cover and simmer 2 hours. Remove cloves and bay leaves; add gingersnaps. Cook 30 minutes, stirring occasionally. When gingersnaps are well broken, serve the meat and gravy, accompanied by **buttered wide noodles** or **fluffy rice**.
6 servings

James Monroe was born April 28, 1758, in Westmoreland Co., Virginia, and was educated privately before entering William and Mary College at the age of 16.

James Monroe

5TH PRESIDENT

1817-1825

Brandy is added to this classic recipe to enhance the dish with a special flavor.

SHORT RIBS OF BEEF, BURGUNDY

4 to 5 pounds beef short ribs
½ cup seasoned flour
¼ cup bacon fat
½ cup chopped onion
1 teaspoon Worcestershire sauce
¼ teaspoon crushed marjoram
¼ teaspoon crushed thyme
1 cup Burgundy
1½ cups beef bouillon
10 to 12 small new potatoes
6 carrots, halved
6 small onions
Salt and pepper
2 tablespoons brandy

Cut beef into 2-inch serving pieces and dredge in seasoned flour. Brown beef on all sides in hot bacon fat, using a heavy kettle or Dutch oven. Add onion and saute until transparent. Stir in Worcestershire, marjoram, thyme, wine, and beef bouillon. Cover tightly and simmer slowly 2 hours or until meat is tender. From time to time, skim excess fat off top of the liquid. Add vegetables and seasonings; simmer until vegetables are tender, about 45 minutes. About 30 minutes before dish is done, add 2 tablespoons brandy, set aflame, and continue cooking after flame has died. *4 servings*

A Frenchman named Lemaire was President Thomas Jefferson's faithful maître d'hôtel and Julien was his chef. They remained with Jefferson when he returned to Monticello, Lemaire acting as the ex-president's steward. Lemaire and Julien carried on at Monticello the tradition of fine cooking that had been developed while Jefferson was at the White House. Here, from Thomas Jefferson's Cookbook by Marie Kimball, is Lemaire's recipe for Beef a la Mode, as tasty today as it was 160 years ago.

Thomas Jefferson's
BEEF A LA MODE

4-pound beef pot roast (top round)
1 onion, finely chopped
1 sprig parsley, finely chopped
½ teaspoon salt
¼ teaspoon ground pepper
⅛ teaspoon grated nutmeg
¼ teaspoon ground thyme
12 strips lean bacon
3 small onions
3 medium carrots
Salt and pepper to taste
¼ teaspoon grated nutmeg
Pinch of ground thyme
4 ounces brandy
1 cup white wine

Take 4 pounds of top of the round and cut off most of the fat. Mix together chopped onion, chopped parsley, salt and pepper, ⅛ teaspoon grated nutmeg, and ¼ teaspoon thyme. Take 4 strips of lean bacon and the fat from the meat, roll in the above mixture and lard the meat with this. Put 4 pieces of bacon into the bottom of your pan (a Dutch oven is best), lay the beef on it and lay on the roast 4 or 5 more strips of bacon. Cut 3 small onions fine, slice 3 carrots, and put into the pot. Add salt and pepper, ¼ teaspoon grated nutmeg, a pinch of thyme, 1 wineglass of brandy, and 1 glass of white wine. Put the pot on a low fire, cover and simmer gently 3 hours, taking care that the meat does not stick to the bottom. Strain the gravy through a fine sieve, skim off the grease and serve. *About 6 servings*

25

Dolly Madison's
BEEF COLLOPS

2½ pounds beef rump
½ cup seasoned flour
2 tablespoons butter
1 pint brown gravy
2 tablespoons butter
  Flour
  Salt and pepper
1 shallot or 3 green onions
27 cucumber pickle slices (4 small
    pickled cucumbers)
1 teaspoon capers, finely cut

Cut thin slices of beef from the rump, or use any other suitable beef cuts, and divide slices into pieces 3 inches long; beat them with the blade of a knife, and flour them. Fry the collops quickly in 2 tablespoons butter 2 minutes, then lay them in a small stew-pan, and cover them with the brown gravy. Add the remaining 2 tablespoons butter rubbed with about 1 tablespoon flour; add salt, pepper, the least bit of shallot shredded as fine as possible, the pickle slices and the capers. (Cover and simmer meat at least an hour, but longer if the meat is a less tender cut. — Editor.) Take care that mixture does not boil before removing meat to a very hot covered serving dish. Bring sauce to boiling, stirring constantly; cook 1 to 2 minutes. Pour over meat.   *4 to 6 servings*

BEEF A LA DEUTSCH

2 tablespoons cooking oil
½ pound fresh mushrooms, sliced
¾ pound white onions, diced
½ pound green peppers, diced
1 small clove garlic, chopped
2 pounds beef round, cut in paper thin strips
  Salt pork, finely chopped
2 cans (16 ounces each) tomatoes or 3 pounds
    fresh tomatoes, chopped
2 tablespoons tomato puree
½ cup chicken broth
⅛ teaspoon black pepper
  Salt to taste
  Dash of oregano

Saute sliced mushrooms in hot cooking oil about 5 minutes, then add the diced onion, green pepper, and chopped garlic; continue cooking over low heat 10 minutes. In a separate skillet, saute meat strips with salt pork pieces until browned. Add meat to the vegetable mixture, then the tomatoes, tomato puree, and chicken broth. Add the pepper, salt, and oregano; cover. Simmer gently for 1 hour, or until meat is fork tender. Serve over **fluffy rice** or **noodles**.

6 servings

The English gave us this dish and its peculiar name — Toad in the Hole. It was very popular around the turn of the century. Round steak was used and cut in a ¼-inch dice. The meat was put in a buttered casserole, covered with a batter and baked. Today, the recipe has been embellished and adapted to modern tastes. It is an especially good recipe to use when you are asked to bring something "potluck."

TOAD IN THE HOLE

½ pound small pork sausage links
1 pound ground beef
½ cup chopped onion
½ cup chopped green pepper
1 small clove garlic, minced
1½ cups canned tomatoes, cut in pieces
  Salt and pepper
¼ cup cornmeal
¼ cup water
¼ cup Burgundy
¾ cup milk
½ teaspoon salt
¼ cup cornmeal
½ cup finely shredded sharp cheddar
    cheese
1 egg, beaten

Place sausages and 1 tablespoon water in a cold skillet. Cover tightly and cook slowly 5 minutes. Remove cover. Pour off drippings and break up sausages. Brown sausages and ground beef in the skillet. Add the onion, green pepper, and garlic; stirring occasionally, cook until onion and pepper are glossy, about 4 minutes. Pour off fat as it collects. Stir in the tomatoes, season with salt and pepper, and add ¼ cup cornmeal mixed with ¼ cup water; then stir in the Burgundy. Cover and let simmer 10 to 15 minutes, stirring occasionally. Turn into a 1½-quart casserole. Make a batter by heating the milk with salt while slowly stirring in another ¼ cup cornmeal. Cook, stirring occasionally, until thickened. Remove batter from heat and stir in the cheese and egg. Pour batter over the meat mixture and bake at 350°F. about 40 minutes or until topping is lightly browned.   *6 servings*

'BURGER SWIRLS WITH MUSHROOM SAUCE

- 1 recipe biscuit dough from a mix
- 2 tablespoons cooking oil
- ¼ cup chopped onion
- ¼ cup chopped celery
- 2 tablespoons chopped green pepper
- 1 pound ground beef (chuck)
- ½ teaspoon salt
- 1 tablespoon meat extract
- ½ cup hot water
- 2 tablespoons flour
  Mushroom Sauce (see recipe)

Prepare biscuit dough but do not bake it; chill it. Meanwhile, heat skillet with a thin film of cooking oil; add vegetables and saute until light brown. Add meat, cutting apart with spoon or fork; cook slightly. Season with salt and mix with vegetables. Dissolve meat extract in water and cool; add flour and shake vigorously in a screwtop jar to blend. Stir into meat mixture; bring to boiling, stirring constantly, and cook 1 to 2 minutes. Cool. Remove chilled biscuit dough from refrigerator and roll out rectangularly, as in making a jelly roll. Spread meat mixture on dough, roll up as for a jelly roll, and seal. Cut roll in 1-inch slices. Put the 'burger swirl slices on a greased baking sheet. Bake at 425°F. 20 minutes, or until golden brown. Serve with Mushroom Sauce spooned over swirls.

4 to 6 servings

Mushroom Sauce

- 1 can (10½ ounces) condensed cream of mushroom soup, undiluted
- ½ teaspoon celery salt
- 1 teaspoon Worcestershire sauce
- 1 teaspoon lemon juice

Combine all ingredients in a saucepan. Heat until sauce attains the degree of **thinness** desired.

About 1¼ cups

Rural life in the early 19th century

Lyndon B. Johnson's
PEDERNALES RIVER CHILI

- 4 pounds ground beef (chuck)
- 1 large onion, chopped
- 2 cloves garlic, minced
- 1 teaspoon ground oregano
- 1 teaspoon cumin seed
- 6 teaspoons chili powder, more if needed
- 2 cans (16 ounces each) tomatoes;
    do not drain
  Salt to taste
- 2 cups hot water

Put meat, onion, and garlic in a large, heavy boiler or skillet. Sear until light colored. Add oregano, cumin, chili powder, tomatoes, salt to taste, and hot water. Bring to boiling. Lower heat and simmer about 1 hour. As fat cooks out, skim. Serve with a side dish of Jalapena peppers. (These are very strong and not at all for people with delicate stomachs.) *About 8 servings*

Salisbury steak was a pre-turn-of-the-century diet fad! And the father of hamburgers. The diet consisted of mincing and broiling meat; eating it 3 times a day, supplemented only with great quantities of water. As a diet it was controversial, but the idea of mincing and later grinding meat quickly caught on. Deviled Salisbury Steak is also a gourmet way to use leftover chicken and turkey meat. Put the cooked poultry through the finest blade of your meat grinder, then substitute it for part of the ground chuck. It is taste appealing!

DEVILED SALISBURY STEAK

- 1½ pounds ground beef (round or chuck)
- ¾ cup herb-seasoned stuffing mix, finely crushed
- ¼ cup chili sauce
- ¼ cup minced onion
- 1 teaspoon salt
- 1 teaspoon prepared horseradish
- 1 teaspoon prepared mustard
- ¼ cup dry red wine or milk

Lightly mix meat with the remaining ingredients until blended. Lightly shape into 1½-inch patties resembling porterhouse steaks. Put on broiler rack and set under broiler with top of meat 3 to 4 inches from source of heat. Broil a total of about 12 minutes, 6 minutes on each side. *4 servings*

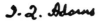

John Quincy Adams—eldest son of the 2nd President, John Adams —was born in Quincy (then part of Braintree), Mass., on July 11, 1767. His birthplace was a house across the yard from, and almost identical with, the house in which his father was born.

ROAST LAMB WITH ELDERBERRY SAUCE

    5 to 7-pound leg of lamb (boned)
    3 cups crumbled corn bread
    ¼ cup minced parsley
    ½ teaspoon salt
      Pinch of pepper
    3 tablespoons mint sauce
    1 egg, beaten
    ¼ cup milk
      Elderberry Sauce (see recipe)

Have meat dealer bone (but not roll) leg of lamb. Fill the cavity with the following stuffing: toss together the crumbled corn bread, parsley, salt and pepper, mint sauce, egg, and milk. Fasten the cavity opening and place lamb on a rack in a shallow roasting pan. Roast 35 minutes to the pound in a 300°-325°F. oven. When ready to serve, slice lamb and pour the Elderberry Sauce over the slices.   *6 to 8 servings*

Elderberry Sauce

    2 tablespoons pan drippings
    1½ tablespoons flour
    ½ teaspoon dry mustard
    ½ cup Burgundy
    ½ cup elderberry jelly
    1 tablespoon mixed grated orange and
      lemon peel

Make a **roux** of the pan drippings and flour. Stir in the dry mustard. Gradually add the wine, stirring constantly. Bring to boiling; cook and stir 1 to 2 minutes. Add the jelly and citrus peel. Heat and stir until jelly is melted and sauce is smooth.   *About 1 cup sauce*

Lamb is listed among the favorite foods of many of our presidents. George Washington's favorite menu of all was a simple one, a piece of mutton and a glass of wine. Many years later, that presidential epicure of the 80's, Chester A. Arthur, chose as his pièce de résistance, a mutton chop and and a glass of ale. The first meal President Kennedy's French chef served to him was not served at the White House. The chef was working in New York's Hotel Carlyle, the hotel Kennedy used as his New York headquarters. His first menu for Kennedy was a packed lunch taken to Kennedy's plane for a flight back to Washington. When reporters asked the chef if the lunch was sandwiches, the chef was indignant. The packed lunch consisted of double lamb chops, mashed potatoes, string beans, and angel food cake.

When the Kennedy clan gathered in Palm Beach with the president for his first Easter dinner as chief of state, the entree was roast lamb jardiniere. That thrifty and industrious wife of a president, Mrs. Rutherford B. Hayes, said jardiniere was the best way of presenting leftover lamb for a second or third meal. Either way it's a delicious dish.

ROAST LEG OF LAMB, JARDINIERE

    6-pound leg of lamb
      Salt and pepper
    1 clove garlic (optional)
    2 small heads cooked cauliflower
   16 stalks cooked asparagus
    8 artichoke bottoms, filled with small
      green peas, heated
    8 sugar-glazed cooked new potatoes
    8 mint-glazed cooked carrots
      Parsley sprig garnish
      Hollandaise sauce for vegetables

Season lamb with salt and pepper; rub with a clove of garlic if you wish. Place the leg, fat side up, on rack in a shallow roasting pan. Insert meat thermometer in fleshy part, away from bone or fat. Roast uncovered in a 300°-325°F. oven until meat thermometer reaches 150° for rare pink, 175° for medium-done, 180° for well-done. Or allow 30 to 35 minutes per pound for roasting. Remove lamb to a heated, extra-large platter and allow to stand 10 minutes. Meanwhile, arrange on platter 2 small, cooked cauliflower heads, asparagus, cooked, artichoke bottoms with peas, sugar-glazed new potatoes, mint-glazed carrots, all heated, and a few sprigs of parsley as garnish. Vegetables should be piping hot, accompanied by a sauceboat of Hollandaise sauce for the cauliflower, asparagus, artichoke-peas.   *8 servings*

Irish stew was a favorite luncheon dish at the White House while McKinley was president. Hanna, the political boss, once announced to McKinley that he knew the president was having Irish stew for lunch because he could smell it. The delicious odors permeating from the White House kitchens drew visitors and tourists. McKinley finally had a glass partition put up to separate the cooks from their public. Here is an Irish stew as McKinley enjoyed it, traditional, and tasty when served with hot biscuits or dumplings.

IRISH STEW FOR 6

3 pounds lean boneless lamb shoulder, cut in
   1½-inch cubes
12 pieces potatoes, large Parisienne
12 pieces onion
12 pieces white turnip
12 pieces carrot
   Salt and pepper to taste
1 bay leaf
1 large Idaho potato, grated

Cover lamb pieces with cold water; bring to a brisk boil. Put in a colander and drain; wash off in cold water; return to a clean stew pot. Add water to cover; simmer meat until half cooked (about 1 hour). Pare and trim vegetables—the traditional cutting shape is a quarter-moon cut, as large as the pieces of meat. Add vegetables, salt, pepper, and bay leaf to pot; and continue cooking until done. Entire cooking time is about 1½ to 2 hours. Add grated potato and cook until it thickens the stew. Remove bay leaf. If necessary, blend in a little flour and water mixture for additional thickening. Cook 1 to 2 minutes.

6 servings

Savory is an herb of the mint family, but it has a delicious flavor all its own. And it does wonders for a roast loin of pork. Use sprigs of parsley and spiced crab apples as a garnish and make a pork loin into a special occasion dinner.

SAVORY BAKED PORK ROAST

3 to 4-pound pork loin roast
1 teaspoon salt
   Pepper to taste
1 tablespoon cornstarch
¼ teaspoon crushed savory
¼ teaspoon ground white pepper
1 can (10½ ounces) condensed consommé,
   undiluted
   Parsley, crab apple garnish

Rub pork loin with salt and pepper. Place meat, fat side up, in a shallow roasting pan, and insert a meat thermometer. Be certain the thermometer does not touch any fat or bone. Roast in a 325°-350°F. oven to an internal temperature of 170°. Cooking times vary, depending upon the amount of fat and bone in the roast, but about 40 minutes per pound is a fair estimate. About 45 minutes before the roast is done, make a basting sauce by mixing cornstarch, savory, and pepper in a saucepan. Add consommé slowly, stirring constantly to blend. Bring to boiling, stirring constantly, and cook 2 to 3 minutes. Spread basting sauce over roast the last 30 minutes of cooking time. Remove roast to a warm platter, garnish with parsley sprigs and hot, spiced crab apples and serve. Pan juices make a delicious gravy.

6 to 8 servings

A combination of the homespun flavor of country pork chops dressed with a continental sauce . . and both easy to fix!

STUFFED PORK CHOPS, BERCY

2 cups corn bread crumbs
3 tablespoons mint sauce
4 pork double rib chops with pocket cut
   on the bone side
   Salt and pepper
1 tablespoon butter
½ cup milk
   Bercy Sauce (see recipe)

Tear corn bread into pieces, and flavor with the mint sauce. Season pork chops and stuff pockets with the minted corn bread. If necessary, skewer or fasten opening. Melt butter in skillet and brown pork chops on both sides. Remove to a casserole and add ½ cup milk. Cover tightly; bake at 350°F. about 1 hour. Remove from oven and discard pan drippings. Serve with the following easy Bercy Sauce.

4 servings

Bercy Sauce

1 tablespoon butter
1 teaspoon minced shallot
2 tablespoons flour
1 cup chicken broth
2 tablespoons chilled butter

Saute shallot in 1 tablespoon butter. Blend in flour; gradually add the chicken broth, stirring constantly. Bring to boiling and cook 1 to 2 minutes. Add the remaining butter, 1 tablespoon at a time, stirring constantly until melted. If desired, stir in a dash of white wine. *1 cup sauce*

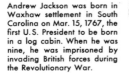

Andrew Jackson was born in Waxhaw settlement in South Carolina on Mar. 15, 1767, the first U.S. President to be born in a log cabin. When he was nine, he was imprisoned by invading British forces during the Revolutionary War.

7TH PRESIDENT

1829-1837

After eight years in the White House, Jackson, ill, returned to the Hermitage, near Nashville, Tenn., to spend his last years quietly, in semi-retirement, as a planter.

Washington held the first presidential barbeque, but LBJ's family popularized it. During Johnson's campaign for election in 1964, the president's daughters, Luci Baines and Lynda Bird, barbequed their way across the country, exhorting "Teen Dems" to work for Johnson. A typical gathering would consume 3,000 biscuits, 1,500 ears of corn, 200 chickens, 800 pounds of beef, and, of course, 400 pounds of LBJ's special Texas-style spareribs.

Along with Washington's favorite Fish House Punch, Arack (Arrack) punch was one of the most popular drinks of colonial America. Arrack, a liquor, was imported from the Indies along with sugar and rum. Thomas Jefferson once accepted some Arrack punch as a legal fee for his services. Add a bottle of Arrack to your husband's liquor cabinet, for it makes delightful drinks in combination with rum. Then borrow a little to make your barbequed ribs original and outstanding. (See also Strawberries in Arrack.)

BARBEQUED RIBS, ARRACK

    4 pounds lean, meaty backribs
    ½ cup Arrack
    1½ cups red wine vinegar
    2 tablespoons salt
    2 tablespoons Worcestershire sauce
    2 cloves garlic, minced
    2 teaspoons celery salt
    2 teaspoons poultry seasoning
    2 tablespoons dry mustard
    1 lemon, sliced thin
    1 large onion, sliced thin

Combine Arrack, vinegar, salt, Worcestershire sauce, garlic, celery salt, poultry seasoning, and dry mustard as a marinade. Cut spareribs into serving pieces and place in marinade for several hours, turning once or twice. Drain marinade and reserve. Place one thinly sliced piece of lemon and one of onion on each piece of ribs. Place meat in a shallow roasting pan, meaty side up, and roast in a 425°F. oven for 45 minutes. Remove from oven and discard lemon and onion. This cooking can be done early and ribs refrigerated until time to "finish" them. Cook the ribs on the barbeque or grill another 30 minutes, turning and basting frequently with marinade to build a flavorful coating.   *4 servings*

Since the reopening of the rebuilt White House in 1818 by President Monroe, the elegant and spacious Blue Room has been used as the main reception room by the President and the First Lady.

President Buchanan's Washington table was set in elegance. But at Wheatland, his Pennsylvania home, he loved to give sauerkraut and mashed potato parties. Surprisingly, the two have a natural affinity. Most men love sauerkraut today . . . and we think most would like this dinner we call

THE BUCHANAN SPECIAL

3½ pounds lean, meaty spareribs
1 pound small pork sausage links
3 cups water
2 cans (27 ounces each) sauerkraut, drained
1 can beer
1 bay leaf
  Pinch of pepper
1 jar (14 ounces) cooked pigs' feet
1 jar (9 ounces) cooked pork hocks

Cut ribs into small serving pieces; brown ribs and sausages in a large kettle or Dutch oven. Remove meat and set aside. Pour off fat, but leave a thin film of fat covering the bottom of the kettle. Add water and sauerkraut; heap spareribs and sausages on top. Pour beer over all. Add bay leaf and pepper and cover. Heat to boiling, then quickly reduce heat and simmer 1½ hours. Add pigs' feet and pork hocks last 30 minutes of cooking time. Remove bay leaf and serve, accompanied by a heaping bowl of **buttered mashed potatoes**. *About 6 servings*

Gourmet Variation

Follow recipe as above, but substitute 1 split (14-ounce bottle) **champagne** for the beer. Instead of serving the dish with mashed potatoes, do this: Drain meat and sauerkraut from the liquid and transfer to a platter in a warm oven. Leave liquid in the kettle and cook these light dumplings.

Dumplings

1 egg
  Milk
1½ cups sifted all-purpose flour
2 teaspoons baking powder
½ teaspoon salt
2 tablespoons melted butter

Break egg into a measuring cup, beat slightly, and add enough milk to fill to the 1-cup line. Sift the flour, baking powder, and salt together into a bowl. Stir in the egg, milk, and melted butter. Drop batter into sauerkraut stock from a wet spoon to make the dumplings. Cover and simmer about 20 minutes. DO NOT lift the lid.

Most of the preparation for this delightful dish can be done ahead of time; the final assembly will take only a few minutes. Completion at the table, using a chafing dish, turns this recipe into real party fare. Or make several "batches" of Sweet and Sour Pork and serve it buffet style to a group.

SWEET AND SOUR PORK

4 tablespoons flour
½ teaspoon salt
2 tablespoons milk
1 egg
1 pound pork tenderloin
½ cup cooking oil
¼ cup cider vinegar
1 can (20 ounces) pineapple chunks; reserve ½ cup syrup
½ teaspoon dry mustard
¼ teaspoon commercially ground orange peel
  Pinch of ground ginger
5 tablespoons brown sugar
1 tablespoon plus 1 teaspoon cornstarch
1 teaspoon salt
1 tablespoon water
1 cup diced green pepper
1 cup coarsely chopped fresh tomato

Blend until smooth the flour, salt, milk, and egg, and let rest for 20 minutes. Cut the pork tenderloin into 2-inch thin strips and dip in the batter; heat the cooking oil and fry the pork strips a few minutes until done. Remove from heat and set aside. In a separate saucepan, combine vinegar and pineapple syrup. Add a mixture of dry mustard, orange peel, ginger, and brown sugar to the liquids. Blend cornstarch and salt with a tablespoon of water and add. Bring to boiling, stirring constantly; cook 2 to 3 minutes. Remove from heat and set aside. Parboil green pepper for 1 minute, then drain and chop. This much of the preparation can be done early and stored until ready to serve (the pork strips refrigerated). A few minutes before serving, or at the table, if you are using a chafing dish, heat some cooking oil, just enough to cover the pan; saute chopped green pepper until glossy. Add the French-fried pork strips, the pineapple chunks, and the sweet and sour sauce. Cover and simmer about 5 minutes. Add the coarsely chopped tomato, re-cover and simmer 2 to 3 minutes. This sweet and sour pork should be spooned over steamed rice. Serve with crusty French bread and a salad. *4 to 6 servings*

For Lenten menus, cooked shrimp can be satis-factorily substituted for the pork.

FRIED RICE WITH PORK JULIENNE

1 cup uncooked rice
2¼ cups water
½ pound pork tenderloin, cut in thin strips
¼ cup cooking oil
1 cup sliced mushrooms
1 medium onion, chopped
1 green pepper, chopped
1¼ cups diced celery
3 chicken bouillon cubes
3 ounces soy sauce
2 egg yolks, slightly beaten

Cook rice in 2¼ cups boiling water, or accord-ing to package directions. While rice is cooking, saute the pork strips in the cooking oil. Then add mushrooms and onion and saute 5 minutes, or until onion is transparent. Add green pepper and celery and cook a few minutes longer. Crum-ble the chicken bouillon cubes into the soy sauce and add to the skillet mixture. Now turn up the heat and add rice, tossing constantly with a spat-ula to prevent sticking. Drizzle egg yolk over mixture while tossing.   *4 to 6 servings*

Lyndon B. Johnson's
FAVORITE CHINESE CHOP SUEY

½ pound lean pork or chicken
2 tablespoons fat
1 cup diced celery
¾ cup diced onion
1 cup chicken bouillon
1 teaspoon salt
¼ teaspoon sugar
¼ cup mushrooms
1 tablespoon cornstarch
2 tablespoons water
2 cans (16 ounces each) bean sprouts, drained
2 cans (16 ounces each) Chinese mixed
    vegetables
Dash each of pepper and paprika

Cut meat into small pieces and brown in fat. Add celery, onion, bouillon, salt, and sugar. Cover and simmer for 20 minutes. Add mush-rooms and paste made of cornstarch and water; bring to boiling and cook 10 minutes, stirring until thickened. Add bean sprouts, mixed vege-tables, and seasonings; heat thoroughly. Serve with **rice** and **crisp noodles.** If desired, 2 table-spoons of soy sauce may be added for additional flavoring.   *About 6 servings*

From Washington to Hoover, Virginia hams have been enjoyed by the presidents. Hoover favored his glazed with a currant sauce. Wash-ington wrote to Lafayette in 1786 that Mrs. Washington had packed and sent to Madame de Lafayette a barrel of Virginia hams and added,"I do not know that they are better, or so good as you make in France, but as they are of our own manu-facture (and you know the Virginia ladies value themselves on the goodness of their bacon) and we recollect that it is a dish of which you are fond, she prevailed on me to ask your's and Madame de Lafayette's acceptance of them." Virginia hams are very salty and have a distinctly different fla-vor than the Midwestern tenderized hams gener-ally found in the food stores.

GLAZED VIRGINIA HAM

1 10-pound Virginia ham
1 onion, quartered
    Sprig of parsley
    A few celery leaves
2 peppercorns
2 green apples
1 bay leaf
1 pint grape juice
1 egg, beaten
½ cup prepared mustard
½ cup brown sugar
    Whole cloves
1 split (14-ounce bottle) champagne
¾ cup pineapple juice

Soak ham in cold water for 24 hours, changing to fresh water several times. Then remove ham and thoroughly wash it under cold running water, scrubbing it well with a stiff brush. Put in a large cooking kettle and add water to gener-ously cover, plus the onion, parsley, celery leaves, peppercorns, quartered apples, bay leaf, and grape juice. Bring to boiling, then reduce heat and simmer ham, covered, until done. Allow about 18 minutes to the pound and keep ham covered in liquid at all times, adding more water, if necessary. Bone can be easily removed when ham is done. Let the ham and the liquid cool to lukewarm, then refrigerate and allow ham to soak in the liquid overnight. The next day remove ham from its liquor, peel off the rind, and trim some of the excess fat. Leave on a very thin film of fat. Brush fat with beaten egg; score in a pattern. Spread with a blend of pre-pared mustard and brown sugar; dot pattern with whole cloves. Bake at 350°F. 30 minutes. Baste frequently with champagne and pineapple juice. Slice paper thin to serve. *About 20 servings*

A variation of an old standby with a sauce that lifts it out of the ordinary.

HAM LOAF WITH CRAB APPLE SAUCE

- ¾ **pound ground ham**
- ¾ **pound ground pork**
- 1 **egg, beaten**
- ½ **cup milk**
- ½ **cup cracker crumbs**
  Milk to cover (about ¼ cup)
  Crab Apple Sauce (see recipe)

Combine ham, pork, egg, milk, and cracker crumbs. Form into a loaf and pack in a 7⅜ x 3⅝ x 2¼-inch loaf pan. Pour milk on top of the loaf to cover. Bake at 350°F. about 1 hour. Pour off excess liquid before serving. Unmold on a serving platter. Spoon some of the Crab Apple Sauce over loaf. Garnish with **spiced crab apple** and **parsley**. Spoon sauce over the ham loaf slices to serve.   *About 6 servings*

Crab Apple Sauce

- 1 **teaspoon dry mustard**
- ¼ **teaspoon ground cinnamon**
- ⅛ **teaspoon ground cloves**
- 3 **tablespoons cider vinegar**
- 1 **jar (10 ounces) crab apple jelly**

Combine all ingredients in a small saucepan. Simmer until jelly is melted, stirring occasionally. Serve hot.   *About 1¼ cups sauce*

President Van Buren was especially fond of ham "washed down with champagne." The following recipe substitutes cider for champagne. It is a colorful dish.

HAM STEAK IN PORT WINE

- 1 **slice smoked ham, 1½ to 2 inches thick**
- 1 **cup sweet cider**
- 1 **cup port**
- ½ **cup maple syrup**
- ½ **cup ground cranberries**
- ½ **cup seedless grapes**
  Juice of 1 orange
- 2 **whole cloves**
  Cornstarch

Place ham in a shallow baking pan. Combine remaining ingredients, except cornstarch, and pour over the ham. Bake at 325°F., allowing 30 minutes per pound of ham. Baste frequently, adding more wine, if necessary. Remove ham and keep warm. Blend 1 or 2 tablespoons cornstarch

with ¼ to ½ cup water. Bring pan drippings to boiling, stirring constantly. Add starch mixture and cook 2 to 3 minutes, continuing to stir. Spoon some gravy over ham before serving.
6 servings

VEAL ZUCCHINI STEW

- 1 **pound veal shoulder, cut in strips**
- 3 **tablespoons grated Parmesan cheese**
- 2 **tablespoons butter**
- 2 **tablespoons cooking oil**
- 4 **small zucchini**
- 2 **small onions, sliced**
- 1 **green pepper, sliced**
- 3 **medium tomatoes**
- ¼ **cup beef bouillon**
  Salt and pepper to taste
- 2 **tablespoons cornstarch**
  Water

Cut veal, then pound flat, pounding Parmesan cheese into the pieces. Saute veal pieces in butter and cooking oil for about 5 minutes. Meanwhile, wash zucchini carefully and slice into ½-inch thick slices; do not pare. Add sliced zucchini to veal and saute a few minutes until zucchini is a delicate brown shade. Then add sliced onion and green pepper and saute about 5 minutes. Peel tomatoes and cut into chunks; add along with ¼ cup beef bouillon or consommé. Season with salt and pepper; cover. Simmer gently 20 minutes. Just before serving thicken the stew with cornstarch made into a paste with a little water; bring to boiling and cook 2 to 3 minutes, stirring constantly.   *4 servings*

8TH PRESIDENT

1837-1841

Martin Van Buren was born in Kinderhook, N.Y., on Dec. 5, 1782. He went to local schools and started to study law at 14. He was admitted to the New York bar in 1803 and soon entered local politics.

One of the many authentic presidential recipes in this book is Mrs. Rutherford B. Hayes' Fricandeau of Veal.

Mrs. Rutherford Hayes'
FRICANDEAU OF VEAL

3-pound veal loin roast
¼ pound salt pork
**4 medium carrots, pared and cut in
   1½-inch slices**
**1 large onion, peeled, quartered and
   stuck with cloves**
1 cup diced celery
2 tablespoons minced parsley
Salt and pepper to taste
Well-buttered parchment paper
**Meat stock (1 can condensed consommé can
   be substituted)**
1 cup boiling water

And this is her recipe: "What is called a fricandeau of veal is simply a cushion of veal trimmed into shape, larded, and braised. Cut a thick slice from a fillet of veal, trim it around as in blind hare (oval shaped) and lard it on top. Put some pieces of pork into a braising kettle, also slices of carrot, an onion with cloves stuck in, a stick of celery, and some parsley. Put in meat, sprinkle over with salt and pepper and cover with well-buttered paper. Now fill the pan with boiling stock, plus water just to cover the meat. Put on a tight lid. If it is a braising pan, set it upon the fire, with live coals on top. If a common saucepan, cover it, and put into a hot oven. It will take about 2½ hours to cook it. A professional cook would boil down the stock in which the fricandeau was cooked until reduced to a glaze, then with a brush would glaze all the top of the meat, placing it in the oven a moment to dry. However, it tastes as well without this extra trouble. The best sauce for a fricandeau is a tomato sauce. It is as often garnished with green peas, spinach or sorrel; or a **roux** may be added to the braising stock for a gravy. The gravy should be strained, of course." It is typical of the cookbooks of Mrs. Hayes' time to leave the finishing of a sauce to the experience and/or the imagination of the cook. We suggest a **tomato sauce** for the fricandeau such as this: Make a roux (paste) of 3 tablespoons of melted butter with 3 tablespoons of flour; stirring constantly, gradually add 1½ cups of stock from the fricandeau, plus 1 can (8 ounces) Spanish-style tomato sauce. Bring to boiling and cook 1 to 2 minutes.

Sharpen with a dash of lemon juice and a dash of Tabasco. The latter is liquid pepper seasoning and has been very popular since President Grant's time.   *About 6 servings*

Grant was first of all a soldier, then a devoted family man, and, official White House entertainments notwithstanding, a man of simple tastes. He was fond of cucumbers, corn, pork and beans, and buckwheat cakes. He would eat only beef, not poultry or game, and his cook learned that the nearer he came to burning up the meat, the better Grant liked it. (If that seems like heresy of sorts today, remember the animals in Grant's day were most indifferently bred.) The authentic recipe for rolled veal from Grant's kitchen is a tasty dish.

Ulysses S. Grant's
VEAL OLIVES

**4 slices (about 1 pound) veal round steak
   (cutlet)**
½ cup bread crumbs
1 tablespoon melted butter
¼ cup chopped onion
¼ teaspoon salt
Pinch of pepper
1 egg, beaten
4 whole cloves
2 tablespoons butter
¼ cup finely chopped onion
¼ cup bread crumbs

Make a stuffing of grated bread crumbs, butter, onion, salt and pepper, and spread over the slices of veal. Beat an egg and spoon over the stuffing; roll each slice up tightly and tie with a thread; stick a clove in each. Grate bread thickly over them after they are put in a skillet with remaining butter and onion. (Brown meat slowly. Add about ½ cup hot water to skillet, cover and simmer about 45 minutes, or until meat is tender. — Editor) When done, lay them on a dish; remove threads and whole cloves. Make your gravy and pour over them. (A delicious gravy can be made by thickening pan drippings with cornstarch and water, while adding, for extra flavor, a crumbled beef bouillon cube; bring to boiling and cook 2 to 3 minutes, stirring constantly. Add 2 tablespoons of sweet vermouth.) The Grant recipe suggests hard-cooked eggs as a garnish.
                              4 servings

William Henry Harrison, born Feb. 9, 1773, at Berkeley plantation on the James River in Virginia, was educated at home. In 1787 he enrolled at Hampden-Sidney College; three years later he went to Richmond, Va., to study medicine, then to Philadelphia to study under noted Dr. Benjamin Rush.

9TH PRESIDENT

1841

Elected President in 1840, Harrison caught cold at his rainy inaugural and died of pneumonia a month after taking office.

This is an unusual and truly gourmet dish . . . if you are an aficionado of kidneys.

SPAGHETTI AMELIO

1 package (½ ounce) dried mushrooms
3-pound roast of veal with kidney
4 medium carrots, pared
4 stalks celery
1 can (28 ounces) tomatoes
1 clove garlic, minced
¼ cup chopped fresh parsley
3 whole bay leaves
3 whole cloves
½ teaspoon basil leaves, crushed
12 ounces very thin spaghetti

Wash mushrooms thoroughly, again and again; put them in a pan of water and bring to boiling. Remove from heat and drain the mushrooms, discarding the water. Add 1 cup fresh water to mushrooms; return to heat and simmer mushrooms until soft. Meanwhile, sear kidney veal roast over high heat. Place roast in a shallow roasting pan and insert meat thermometer in it. Add carrots and celery to pan and roast in a 325°F. oven. Into a large bowl put the tomatoes, cooked mushrooms, that have been chopped fine, and the stock they were cooked in, plus the garlic, parsley, bay leaves, cloves, and crushed basil. After the meat has cooked an hour, add the tomato stock to the pan drippings and return to oven. Cook until meat thermometer registers 170°F. Remove meat from pan and keep warm. Discard celery and bay leaves. Pour sauce into a saucepan, reserving carrots. Mash carrots and add to sauce. Simmer sauce 30 minutes, skimming fat from time to time. Last 10 minutes, put spaghetti into plenty of boiling salted water and cook until tender; drain. Toss spaghetti with sauce and serve immediately, accompanied by slices of the roast. *6 to 8 servings*

VEAL PICCATA

2 pounds veal round steak (cutlet), cut in thin, 3-inch slices
Parmesan cheese
Lemon juice
Soy sauce
Herb-seasoned stuffing mix, finely crushed
½ cup butter
2 cloves garlic, bruised
Pinch of ground thyme, a generous one
2 whole lemons, sliced as thinly as possible
1½ cups sliced fresh mushrooms

With a meat cleaver, pound meat pieces as thin as possible, at the same time pounding in some freshly grated Parmesan cheese. Sprinkle meat pieces with lemon juice and soy sauce; then coat in herb-seasoned stuffing mix. Let rest 20 minutes. Melt ¼ cup of the butter in a skillet to which a bruised clove of garlic and the thyme have been added. Saute the coated meat in butter until lightly browned on both sides. In another skillet, melt other ¼ cup butter to which other bruised clove of garlic has been added. Saute lemon slices for a few minutes, then add sliced, fresh mushrooms and saute 5 minutes. Discard garlic clove from each skillet; combine all the ingredients. Scrape meat drippings and combine with other pan drippings. Entend with a little white wine (optional) and pour over meat. Serve accompanied by rice. *4 servings*

Parmigiano is Italian for Parmesan cheese, and Parmesan cheese has been around America for a long time. John Adams, our second president, utilized his diaries to record menus of dinners he had enjoyed, and Parmesan cheese was often mentioned as being served. That was before 1800. Parmesan cheese works well in concert with veal and can be made into a casserole to be prepared early and baked later.

CASSEROLE OF VEAL PARMIGIANO

1½ pounds thin veal round steak (cutlet)
 1 cup grated Parmesan cheese
 2 eggs, beaten
   Salt and pepper
1¼ cups herb-seasoned stuffing mix, finely crushed
 5 oz. fresh mushrooms
 3 tablespoons butter, heated in a skillet
¼ cup olive or cooking oil
 1 can (10½ ounces) condensed tomato soup, undiluted
 1 can (8 ounces) Spanish-style tomato sauce
 1 tablespoon sugar
½ cup sauterne
 1 package (6 ounces) mozzarella cheese slices

Cut veal into fairly large pieces. Pound thin, at the same time pounding Parmesan cheese into the pieces. Beat 2 eggs with a little salt and pepper. Dip cutlets into the egg and then into the finely crushed seasoned stuffing mix. Let cutlets rest in refrigerator for 10 minutes while slicing and sauteing the fresh mushrooms in the butter. Remove veal from refrigerator and saute in cooking oil about 5 minutes on each side. Place cooked veal in a shallow casserole; combine tomato soup, tomato sauce, sugar, and wine; pour over veal. Top with slices of mozzarella cheese. Heat in a 300°F. oven for 30 minutes. When the cheese had browned slightly and the sauce is bubbling, casserole is ready to be served.

4 to 6 servings

The state dinner the Kennedys gave on February 21, 1962 was ostensibly in honor of then Vice President Lyndon B. Johnson, House Speaker John W. McCormack, and Chief Justice (Supreme Court) Earl Warren. But the guest of honor, in absentia, seemed to be John H. Glenn Jr., America's first astronaut to orbit the earth. Glenn was the talk of the glittering party, and the subject of many toasts. Featured on the French banquet menu was an elegant French dish, filet of veal in aspic. The classic preparation of meat aspics usually involves foie gras, truffles, special sauces, et cetera. A much easier veal dish to prepare is a decorated veal loaf in a mold, an appealing dish to serve guests.

TIMBALE OF VEAL WITH HORSERADISH CREAM

 2 pounds lean, ground veal
 4 slices fresh bread
½ cup chicken stock
¼ cup shredded American cheese
½ cup heavy cream
   Pinch of white pepper
 1 egg, beaten
   Salt to taste
 1 tablespoon finely chopped shallots, sautéed lightly in butter
¼ cup sliced ripe olives
¼ cup sliced pimiento-stuffed olives
   Horseradish Cream (see recipe)

Heavily butter a 1-quart timbale mold and chill in the refrigerator before using. Soak bread in the chicken stock, then whip with fork. Mix lightly with all remaining ingredients, except olives. Remove timbale mold from the refrigerator and line the side and bottom with olive slices, ripe and green, in a decorative pattern. Then carefully press a layer of meat mixture against the olives so that the olives don't pull away from the sides of the mold. (Buttered fingers facilitate this preparation.) Fill center of the mold with remaining meat mixture. Place mold in a pan of hot water. Bake at 350°F. 1½ hours. Unmold carefully onto serving platter. Accompany with Horseradish Cream.

6 to 8 servings

Horseradish Cream

¼ cup whipped cream
¼ cup mayonnaise
 2 teaspoons prepared horseradish
 1 teaspoon lemon juice

Blend all ingredients.

Abigail Adams was the first First Lady to actually live in the new White House (1800). Though just erected, it was a desolate barn of a place, almost inaccessible to the muddy, swampy village of Washington. Abigail described the trial of establishing housekeeping there as most inconvenient. One of her first visitors was a Mt. Vernon servant with a congratulatory note from the Washingtons and a big haunch of venison for the somewhat sparse White House larder. Though a luxury food today, venison was a staple item in colonial America. The earliest colonists subsisted almost entirely on wild game and wild fowl. What is now known as West Virginia and eastern Ohio harbored not only deer and bear, but also, big horned sheep and buffalo, animals we associate with the Far West today. George Washington, when working as a surveyor and also as an army officer in West Virginia, enjoyed big horn sheep and buffalo—the delicacy was the buffalo hump! Venison was quite tastefully prepared, too. Early recipes called for baking venison in butter with a wine sauce, or using lemon juice and currants as a garnish.

President Lyndon Johnson was the most avid big game hunter since Teddy Roosevelt. One of his favorite recreations was hunting deer on the 5,000 acres he owned and leased in central Texas.

Venison, being wild game, is subject to toughness in older animals. Their meat can be tenderized by marinating in a vegetable-wine marinade. If you are lucky enough to have some meat from a fawn or younger animal, here is a recipe for preparing venison. Elk, antelope, or moose (young moose tastes more like beef than game) may be substituted for the deer if they are available.

BRAISED VENISON IN SOUR CREAM

    2 pounds venison
    ¼ cup diced salt pork
    1 clove garlic, bruised
    1 cup diced celery
    1 cup diced carrot
    ¼ cup minced onion
    1 bay leaf
    1 cup water
    ¼ cup butter
    ¼ cup flour
    1 cup dairy sour cream

Cut venison into 2-inch pieces; put salt pork into a heavy skillet. Add meat and garlic; brown on all sides. Arrange in ovenproof casserole. Put vegetables in remaining fat in the skillet and cook 2 minutes, or until soft. Season with **salt** and **pepper**; add bay leaf and water. Pour over the meat in the casserole. Cover and cook in a 325°F. oven until meat is tender. It is difficult to specify cooking times for wild game. It all depends on the age of the animal. The older the animal, the longer the cooking period. Allow at least 1½ hours, probably more. Melt butter in a skillet and stir in flour. Gradually add juices that the meat was cooked in, stirring until smooth. Boil 1 to 2 minutes. Remove bruised garlic clove from the casserole. At the last minute, add sour cream in small amounts, continuing to stir; heat gently but do not boil. Spoon sauce over meat and vegetables. Garnish with currant jelly and serve with buttered noodles.

4 servings

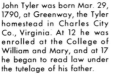

John Tyler was born Mar. 29, 1790, at Greenway, the Tyler homestead in Charles City Co., Virginia. At 12 he was enrolled at the College of William and Mary, and at 17 he began to read law under the tutelage of his father.

10TH PRESIDENT

1841-1845

In 1861 Tyler was elected to the provisional Congress of the Confederacy. He died the following year.

Poultry

. . . wherein Thomas Jefferson discusses turkey

BRILLAT-SAVARIN, WHO FLED TO EXILE in America during the French Revolution, was considered the world's greatest authority on gastronomy by his contemporaries. In America he was a close friend of our great gourmet President, Thomas Jefferson. And the American dish that made the most impression on Savarin was the colonials' roasted wild turkey. Europeans had domesticated poultry, but wild turkey was indigenous to the Americas.

It was only natural that turkey was a favorite of many of our presidents. Andrew Jackson's favorite food was turkey hash. But it was more of a gruel than a hash. It would be called a thin fricassee of turkey today, and much too plain for modern tastes. Newly elected President Franklin D. Roosevelt visited Jackson's estate, The Hermitage, in 1933. The chef, wanting to serve something elegant, to F. D. R. added Worcestershire sauce to spruce up the original recipe, and prepared Andrew Jackson's turkey hash. Here is that recipe:

Andrew Jackson's
TURKEY HASH

Prepare a medium-sized (8 to 10 pounds) **turkey** for a roaster; add sufficient water to make stock: put **celery, onion,** a **bay leaf, salt,** pod or two of **red pepper** in water. Cover; allow to cook slowly until tender; do not brown. Pour and strain off stock; allow to cool. When fat rises to top, skim off—but do not use. When turkey has cooled, pull apart, discarding all skin, bones, and gristle; cut in fairly large, bite-size pieces. Make the sauce by heating 4 tablespoons **butter** in a large skillet or saucepan and blending in 2 tablespoons **flour** until smooth. Heat until bubbly. Stirring constantly, add gradually a quart of the turkey stock. Bring to boiling and cook 1 to 2 minutes. Season with **Worcestershire sauce;** to each quart of sauce add 2 quarts of cut-up turkey. Serve very hot from a double boiler. (In those days a **bain marie** would have been used.) Add white pepper, if needed.

NOTE: To prepare less than 2 quarts, cook a smaller portion of sauce and cut up enough turkey in proportion to the amount of sauce used and the desired number of servings. Leftover turkey may be used for other food preparation.

It was during President Grant's administration (in 1869) that a forward-thinking turkey entrepreneur hit upon the idea of sending a turkey to his neighbor in the White House. Grant received a whopping 36-pound Rhode Island turkey from the state famous for its poultry. Mr. Vose, the turkey grower, sent Christmas turkeys to all of the presidents from Grant through Teddy Roosevelt. Roosevelt's was a more modest 26-pound turkey. The White House released the recipe for Roosevelt's Christmas turkey that "plain and sensible" recipes might be available to all. The released recipe was for stuffing an 18-pound bird.

Teddy Roosevelt's
CHRISTMAS TURKEY

1 dozen large **oysters,** minced very fine; 2 cupfuls of **fine bread crumbs,** a tablespoonful of chopped **herbs** (parsley, thyme or sweet marjoram), and a sparing amount of **salt** and **pepper.** Stuff turkey; roast.

When you take turkey, the second most American food, and combine it with corn, the first most American food, you have a marriage of delightful flavors. Here is a truly American dish, roast turkey with colonial johnnycake stuffing.

ROAST TURKEY WITH CHEF'S STUFFING

    4 cups crumbled johnnycake
      Turkey giblets, neck
    3 chicken bouillon cubes
    1 quart water
      Celery leaves
  ½ teaspoon salt
  ¼ teaspoon dry mustard
    1 pound chestnuts
  ½ pound small pork sausage links
  ½ pound butter
    2 tablespoons lemon juice
    1 cup chopped onion
    1 cup chopped celery
  ¼ cup chopped parsley
  ½ teaspoon whole sage
    1 teaspoon crushed rosemary
    1 teaspoon crushed marjoram
    1 teaspoon crushed basil
    1 teaspoon crushed thyme
      Salt and pepper
    1 cup turkey stock
  ½ pound unsalted butter
      Parchment paper
      14-pound turkey

Combine ingredients for the turkey stock (giblets, neck, bouillon cubes, water, celery leaves, salt, and mustard), bring to a quick boil, then reduce heat and simmer, covered, until giblets are cooked tender. Discard turkey neck; reserve giblets for gravy if you wish. Strain stock through cheesecloth or fine sieve and reserve. Cut a gash in the tough outer skin of the chestnuts; boil them and when cooked, peel and chop them fine. Parboil sausages until cooked, but do not brown them; cool and crumble. Melt ½ pound butter in a large skillet, add 2 tablespoons lemon juice and saute onion and celery until soft but not browned. Combine the crumbled johnnycake with parsley, herbs, and seasonings; toss lightly. Add chopped, cooked chestnuts and sausage meat. Stir mixture into skillet with celery and onion, and stir until all the butter is absorbed. Moisten dressing with 1 cup of turkey stock. Loosely pack stuffing into cavities of the turkey. Skewer or sew up opening and truss bird. Rub skin with some unsalted butter. Melt the remaining butter and butter well parchment paper. Place turkey on a rack in a shallow roasting pan. Lay buttered parchment paper on top of turkey. Roast in a 325°F. oven until done. (During roasting period brush turkey with the melted butter and re-cover with the parchment paper. — Editor)   *About 14 servings*

Pat Nixon's

CHESTNUT AND APPLE STUFFING

    2 slices bacon, chopped
    1 tablespoon butter
    1 cup *each* chopped celery and onion
    6 cups fresh white bread cubes
    4 cups coarsely chopped boiled chestnuts
    4 cups chopped pared cored apples
  ½ cup raisins
    1 tablespoon *each* salt, poultry seasoning, and chopped parsley
    2 eggs
    1 cup warm milk

Render the bacon in a large skillet. Add the butter, celery, and onion; saute until tender, about 5 minutes. Mix lightly in a large bowl with remaining ingredients — add eggs and milk last — until well combined.
Stuffing for a 10- to 12-pound turkey

President Grant's daughter Nellie was married to Algernon Sartoris in a lavish and picturesque White House wedding in the East Room.

President John Adams, in his diaries, mentioned serving his guests Indian pudding. It was served as a first course with plenty of molasses and butter. He told of serving bacon, neck of mutton, veal, and vegetables, and of his enjoyment of a dinner spiced with punch, wine, porter, beer, and especially, Parmesan cheese. He enjoyed whortleberry (a relative of the huckleberry) puddings, and especially stewed cranberries and goose on a spit. If you have a spit on your barbeque, try roasting a goose similar to the way it was done in John Adams' time. In his day, small boys were obliged to keep the spit turning manually. With the electric motors of today, it's easy to have a tasty, nonfatty roast goose!

GOOSE ON A SPIT

1 10-pound goose
1 clove garlic, bruised
½ cup Madeira
   Salt and pepper
1 orange, quartered
1 tart apple, quartered
1 pared potato, quartered
3 cups hot water
1 pound bulk pork sausage
1 cup chopped onion
1 cup chopped celery
2 cups herb-seasoned stuffing mix
1 cup stock
¾ cup orange juice

Wash, clean, and pat the goose dry, inside and out. Rub outside gently with the garlic; discard garlic. Rub in Madeira, outside and inside. Sprinkle inside with salt and pepper. Put orange, apple, and potato pieces inside the body cavity. Place goose in a large covered pan or electric roaster, and add 3 cups hot water. Steam, covered, for 1 hour. While goose is steaming, brown pork sausage, add onion and celery and cook until soft but not brown. Let cool. Remove goose from roaster after an hour, and discard orange, apple, and potato. Remove 1 cup of stock from pan. (Remaining stock may be discarded or used for gravy.) Soften stuffing mix in the stock; add orange juice. Toss stuffing with cooked sausage, celery, and onion. Lightly stuff goose cavities; skewer and truss bird securely so no stuffing escapes while bird is on the spit. Have charcoal white hot; follow rotisserie manufacturer's directions for regulating temperature. Place the goose on the spit and prick holes all over the skin (to let excess fat drip out). Roast on a turning spit about 2½ hours, keeping the charcoal hot. During cooking, prick goose skin to let fat drip out. The length of cooking time varies according to the degree of heat. Test for doneness by moving the drumstick up and down; the joints should yield readily or twist out and the drumstick meat should feel very soft. To serve, remove skewers and cord; place on a warm serving platter and garnish as desired. *6 to 8 servings*

James Knox Polk was born in Mecklenburg Co., North Carolina, Nov. 2, 1795. His family moved to Tennessee in 1806. After graduation from the University of North Carolina in 1818, Polk studied law.

11TH PRESIDENT

1845-1849

Polk entered Congress in 1825 and in 1835 was chosen Speaker of the House as a reward for party loyalty.

A favorite Kennedy dinner menu released by the White House included Iced Tomato Soup, Chicken Breasts with Noodles, String Beans Amandine, and Gâteau St. Honoré with Demitasse. The following recipe for the entree mentioned is a good party dish, but is definitely NOT for the calorie conscious. Parts of this long recipe can be done ahead of time; even so, it takes quite a bit of preparation. This is a rather expensive dish. We suggest, for home consumption, you cut the amount of fresh mushrooms called for in half.

WHITE HOUSE CHICKEN BREASTS WITH NOODLES

    8 whole chicken breasts, flattened
      Salt and pepper to taste
      Dash of crushed marjoram
      Butter to cover skillet
    3 pounds fresh mushrooms
    ½ pound butter
   12 ounces noodles
    2 tablespoons butter
    2 cups basic white sauce
    1 cup cold milk
    1 cup chicken stock
      White House Hollandaise Sauce (see recipe)
    ½ cup dry white wine
      Parmesan cheese, grated

Season chicken breasts with salt, pepper, and marjoram. Saute in butter until breasts are fully cooked. While chicken is cooking, wash mushrooms and cut into small pieces, then saute in ½ pound of butter. Cook noodles until done; drain and work 2 tablespoons of butter gently into the noodles. Make 2 cups of basic white sauce; add to it the cold milk and chicken stock. Cook mixture until thickened. Reserve while making White House Hollandaise Sauce. Carefully blend Hollandaise with the white sauce mixture; stir in dry white wine. Butter a casserole. (That's the way the White House recipe reads; however, they are using professional equipment. For home adaptation you will do best to use your small, covered roasting pan.) After buttering, place noodles in the bottom; add the mushrooms and place chicken breasts on top of the mushrooms. Pour the sauce over all. Heat thoroughly in a 325°F. oven about 45 minutes. Remove from oven, sprinkle with grated Parmesan cheese and place under broiler to brown.   *8 servings*

NOTE: This recipe may be increased to include 12 chicken breasts without changing the other ingredients.

White House Hollandaise Sauce

    4 egg yolks
    ½ cup cream
    2 tablespoons lemon juice
    4 tablespoons cold butter

Beat the egg yolks in the top of a double boiler, then beat in the cream. Cook and stir over hot water until slightly thickened. Blend in the lemon juice. Cut in the butter a tablespoon at a time. Sauce will further thicken.
About 1 cup sauce

CHICKEN DRUMSTICKS, BOURGUIGNONNE

      Red Wine Marinade (see recipe)
   12 large chicken drumsticks
    ½ cup seasoned flour
    ¼ cup cooking oil
    2 cups Basic Brown Sauce (page 80)
      Salt and pepper
      Bourguignonne Sauce (see recipe)

Marinate chicken drumsticks in Red Wine Marinade for TWO DAYS. Remove drumsticks and reserve marinade. Dredge chicken pieces in flour seasoned with salt and pepper. Saute drumsticks in oil until brown. Place drumsticks in a buttered 5-quart casserole or covered roasting pan. Pour over them the brown sauce to which 1 cup of the strained marinade has been added; salt and pepper to taste. Cover and bake at 325°F. 1 hour. Drain chicken and place on a warm platter while making Bourguignonne Sauce. Pour sauce over drumsticks.   *6 servings*

Red Wine Marinade

    2 cups red wine
    ¼ cup finely diced carrot
    ¼ cup finely diced celery
    ¼ cup finely diced onion
    1 tablespoon mixed pickling spices

Add vegetables and spices to wine; mix well.

Bourguignonne Sauce

    ¼ cup cooking oil
    ¼ cup finely diced salt pork
    ¼ cup finely diced mushrooms
      Strained sauce from casserole
    ¼ cup pearl onions

Fry salt pork and mushrooms in cooking oil 5 minutes; drain. Add salt pork and mushrooms along with onions to the strained sauce. Bring quickly to boiling and pour over drumsticks.

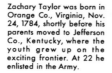

Zachary Taylor was born in Orange Co., Virginia, Nov. 24, 1784, shortly before his parents moved to Jefferson Co., Kentucky, where the youth grew up on the exciting frontier. At 22 he enlisted in the Army.

12TH PRESIDENT

1849-1850

Shortly before Taylor's death in 1850 after 16 months as President, Henry Clay made his moving plea in the Senate for compromise between North and South.

And still another easy version of one of America's favorites . . . fried chicken.

OVEN FRIED CHICKEN WITH CREOLE SAUCE

    1 3½-pound chicken, cut in pieces,
         or 10 to 14 chicken pieces
       Seasoned flour
    ½ cup evaporated milk
    1½ cups corn flake crumbs
       Creole Sauce (see recipe)

Dip chicken pieces in seasoned flour, then milk; roll in corn flake crumbs. Coat evenly and let rest 10 minutes. Line a large, shallow baking pan with foil and loosely pack in the chicken pieces, skin side up. Start in a 425°F. oven for 10 minutes; turn down to 325°F. until done, about 45 minutes. It is not necessary to turn chicken or to cover it, even for a partial time. Make the Creole Sauce and spoon over pieces.   *About 6 servings*

Creole Sauce

    ½ cup cooking oil
    1 cup chopped onion
    1 cup chopped green pepper
    1 can (16 ounces) tomatoes
    ¼ cup tomato sauce
    1 teaspoon Worcestershire sauce
    ½ teaspoon salt
    1 teaspoon celery salt
    1 teaspoon seasoned salt
    1 teaspoon sugar
    ½ teaspoon chili powder
    2 tablespoons flour

Heat oil in a saucepan. Add the onion and green pepper and saute until glossy. Stir in the tomatoes, tomato sauce, and seasonings. Bring to boiling. Meanwhile, pour ¼ to ½ cup water into a screw-top jar, add the flour, and shake it vigorously. Stir into sauce and boil 1 to 2 minutes; cover and simmer for 30 minutes.

2 cups sauce

STUFFED CORNISH HENS, VERONIQUE

    4 Rock Cornish game hens
    ¼ pound softened butter
    ½ cup chopped onion
    3 cups crumbled johnnycake
       Salt and pepper
    ½ teaspoon celery salt
    ½ cup minced parsley
       Juice of 1 lemon
       Pat of unsalted butter
       Veronique Sauce (page 82)

Saute onion in butter until soft, but not browned; remove from heat. Add corn bread, salt and pepper, celery salt, parsley, and lemon juice; mix thoroughly. Loosely stuff the cavities of hens with the corn bread mixture. Pull loose skin over cavity openings; fasten with skewer. Fasten neck skin to back with a skewer; tie wings and legs to body. Brush with unsalted butter. Place, breast side up, in a roasting pan and roast in a 400°F. oven about 1 hour, basting with pan drippings. Spoon some Veronique Sauce over birds before serving.   *4 servings*

In one of the two early cookbooks favored by Martha Washington, there is an interesting recipe for a chestnut stuffed capon. The recipe is just as practical today with one exception. Martha's book's "receipt" called for roasting the fowl this way: "The best way of doing it (the fowl) is to tie the neck and hang it up by the legs to roast with a string and baste it with butter." We'll pop this tasty bird into a well regulated oven, but the ingredients for the stuffing and sauce are authentic and unchanged. There are no bread crumbs in this stuffing. None are needed, due to the nature of the chestnuts.

CHESTNUT STUFFED CAPON, MT. VERNON STYLE

1 6-pound capon
1 pound chestnuts
¼ pound ham or bacon (cooked)
½ cup chopped parsley
   Pinch sweet herbs (rosemary, marjoram)
¼ teaspoon ground mace
   Salt and pepper to taste
¼ teaspoon ground nutmeg
2 tablespoons unsalted butter

First, roast chestnuts very carefully, so as not to burn them; take off the skin and peel them; take about a dozen of them, cut small, and bruise them in a mortar; parboil the liver of the capon, bruise it, cut about a quarter of a pound of ham or bacon, and pound it; then mix them all together with a good deal of parsley, chopped small, a little sweet herbs, some mace, pepper, salt, and nutmeg. Mix these together and put into your capon and roast it (allow 25 to 30 minutes per pound at 325°F.). The best way of doing it is to tie the neck, and hang it up by the legs to roast with a string, and baste it with butter. For sauce, take the remaining chestnuts; put them into some good gravy with a little white wine, and thicken it with a piece of butter rolled in flour; then take up your capon, lay it in the dish, and pour in the sauce. Garnish with lemon.

6 to 8 servings

BREAST OF CHICKEN SAVANNAH

4 large chicken breasts, split
2½ ounces (about ¼ cup) peanut butter
8 thin slices cooked ham
¼ cup sherry
   Parmesan Sauce (see recipe)

Lift skin on chicken breasts slightly, and spread a film of peanut butter on meat under skin; replace skin. Place 1 slice of cooked ham over skin side of each breast. Put ¼ cup sherry in a large casserole or braising pan. Add chicken pieces, ham side up; cover and bake at 350°F. 1 hour or until pieces are tender. Remove breasts from pan and keep warm while preparing Parmesan Sauce. Pour sauce over chicken and serve.

8 servings

Parmesan Sauce

¼ cup pan drippings
¼ cup flour
2 cups milk, scalded
½ teaspoon salt
6 tablespoons freshly grated
   Parmesan cheese
2 tablespoons iced butter

Put the pan drippings into a medium saucepan. Add flour and stir, while heating until bubbly. Add milk gradually, stirring well; bring to boiling and cook 1 to 2 minutes. Add salt and Parmesan cheese, stirring until cheese melts. Stir in butter, 1 tablespoon at a time.

About 2 cups sauce

CHICKEN BREASTS, CHANTILLY

1 large clove garlic, pressed
1 cup heavy cream
4 chicken breasts, butterflied
   Salt and pepper to taste
¼ cup fine dry bread crumbs
¼ cup cooking oil
1 cup half and half cream
½ cup sliced ripe olives
4 sprigs parsley

Add pressed garlic to 1 cup heavy cream and let stand 30 minutes so flavors marry. Remove garlic. Season chicken with salt and pepper and dredge in fine dry bread crumbs; let rest 20 minutes. Heat oil in frying pan and brown chicken on both sides. Remove chicken and place in buttered casserole. Pour half and half and heavy cream over chicken breasts. Cover and bake at 350°F. 1 hour or until chicken is fork tender. Place chicken on serving plates. Add ripe olives to cream sauce, and spoon some sauce over each piece. Garnish with a sprig of parsley.

4 servings

NOTE: If desired, after chicken has baked about 30 minutes, add 1 package (10 ounces) frozen peas, gently broken up a bit to separate; continue baking about 30 minutes.

Chicken Kiev is reputedly Czarist in origin. It has become a popular feature of better restaurants in recent years. Chicken Kiev is made from chicken breasts with the first joint of the shoulder bone left on. When properly constructed, they resemble plump little boats with a little mast sticking up. Once made, do not bruise or penetrate with a fork while deep fat frying or serving.

CHICKEN KIEV

Breasts of 3 3-pound chickens, boned
    and skinned with first shoulder
    joint left on
Bourguignonne Butter (see recipe)
1 cup flour, seasoned with salt and
    pepper
Egg wash
Flour
3 cups fresh white bread crumbs
Deep fat for frying, heated to 375°F.

One half breast with first joint of shoulder bone left on is one portion. Flatten the breast and attached filet with meat cleaver. Stuff each chicken breast with Bourguignonne Butter; fold the filet over the butter and roll breast over filet, making a cone-shaped piece with shoulder bone sticking up. Dip the stuffed breast in flour, egg wash (4 eggs, beaten, in ½ cup water) and white bread crumbs. Let rest 10 minutes, dip again in egg wash and bread crumbs. Fry in hot fat 10 minutes or until done. *6 servings*

Bourguignonne Butter

½ pound unsalted butter, softened
4 drops Worcestershire sauce
3 drops Tabasco
1 tablespoon finely chopped chives
1½ cups white bread crumbs
1 tablespoon minced shallots

Mix butter, Worcestershire, Tabasco, chives, bread crumbs, and shallots that have been very lightly sauteed. Chill butter.

A Southern plantation dinner used to mean a barbeque, plus burgoo and/or Brunswick stew. The favorite stew ingredient was squirrel meat. Other Southerners claim the original Brunswick stew had a chicken base. Which came first, the chicken or the squirrel, has been lost in the culinary mists of great, great, great grandmother's day. We have chosen chicken because it is readily available. If you wish to substitute squirrel, clean and dress 4 or 5 squirrels to one 4-pound chicken. Here's yet another version of

BRUNSWICK STEW

1 4-pound chicken, disjointed
¼ cup cooking oil
1 cup coarsely chopped onion
¼ pound salt pork, chopped
4 tomatoes, peeled and quartered
2 cups boiling water
1 cup sherry
1 bay leaf
1 teaspoon Worcestershire sauce
1½ cups fresh lima beans
½ cup sliced fresh okra
1½ cups fresh bread crumbs
2 tablespoons butter
    Salt to taste

Saute chicken in cooking oil until golden brown; remove chicken. Brown onion and salt pork in the same fat. Put chicken, salt pork, onion, tomatoes, boiling water, sherry, bay leaf, and Worcestershire sauce in Dutch oven or stew pot. Cover and simmer 2 hours, or until chicken is tender. After 1 hour, remove bay leaf; add 1½ cups fresh lima or butter beans and cook about 15 minutes. Add ½ cup sliced fresh okra; continue cooking about 15 minutes. Stir in fresh bread crumbs that have been sauteed in butter. Add salt to taste before serving. *8 servings*

Railroad magnates carried the elegance of Eastern entertaining to California, as evidenced by this sumptuous banquet for ex-president Grant being traditionally honored by a railroad financier at his colorful Nob Hill home in San Francisco.

Coq au Vin (chicken in wine) is a rich, hearty French peasant dish and easily prepared at home.

COQ AU VIN

    2 tablespoons butter
    2 tablespoons cooking oil
    ¾ cup chopped green onion
    ¼ pound salt pork, diced fine
    8 disjointed chicken pieces
    ½ cup flour
      Salt and pepper
    2 ounces brandy
    1 clove garlic, pressed
    1 bouquet garni
   12 mushrooms, peeled and sliced
    2 cups red wine

Melt butter in a skillet and add cooking oil (to keep butter from scorching). Saute onion in it until transparent; add salt pork and brown. Remove pork and onion from skillet and reserve. In the remaining fat gently brown the chicken pieces that have been dredged in flour and seasoned with salt and pepper. Drain off excess fat, if any. Warm 2 ounces of brandy; pour over the chicken pieces and set aflame. When brandy has burned out, add the following to the chicken pieces: the pork and onion, garlic, the **bouquet garni** (1 bay leaf, stalk of celery with leaves left on, sprig of parsley, and a pinch each of thyme and rosemary tied in cheesecloth), the peeled, sliced mushrooms, and 2 cups of red wine. Cover and simmer an hour or until chicken is done. Remove **bouquet garni** and garlic. Sauce may be thickened for a "gravy" or merely strained and poured over chicken pieces as pan juices.

4 servings

KENTUCKY FRIED CHICKEN

    ½ cup flour
      Salt and Pepper
   12 chicken pieces or a 3½-pound
      broiler-fryer, cut in pieces
    ¼ pound butter or margarine
    ¼ cup bourbon whiskey
    ¼ cup water

Blend salt and pepper with flour and coat chicken pieces. Cover skillet with a thin film of cooking oil. Melt butter or margarine in skillet and add chicken pieces. Add bourbon and brown chicken pieces in butter and bourbon over medium heat. Add water; cover and simmer 45 minutes. Remove cover and cook 15 minutes.

4 to 6 servings

FRENCH FRIED CHICKEN WITH CORN CHIPS

    1 egg, beaten
    ½ teaspoon salt
    1 tablespoon water
   2½-pound broiler-fryer chicken, disjointed
    ¾ cup corn chips, crushed finely
    6 cups peanut oil, heated to 350°F.

Combine egg, salt, and water. Dip chicken pieces first in the egg, then in the crushed corn chips. Let rest in the refrigerator 1 hour. Fry chicken pieces in hot deep fat; time will vary from 15 to 25 minutes depending on size of pieces. Drain first batch of pieces on absorbent paper while frying second batch; keep hot. *4 servings*

Smothered chicken and dressing is a great American favorite, and the following recipe for it is both rich and wholesome.

SMOTHERED CHICKEN, ILLINOIS STYLE

    2 broiler-fryer chickens, cut in pieces
   2½ cups water
    1 teaspoon salt
    1 small onion, chopped
    1 cup celery tops
    ½ cup seasoned flour
    ¼ cup cooking fat
    1 loaf bread, crusts trimmed, cut in
      ½-inch cubes
    1 teaspoon salt
    ¼ teaspoon pepper
   1½ teaspoons ground sage
    1 small onion, grated
    ½ cup melted butter
    ¼ cup flour
   1½ cups cream

Place giblets, necks, and backs in water; add salt, onion, and celery tops to pan. Cover and simmer 1 hour; remove meat from bones and strain the broth. Dredge remaining chicken pieces in flour seasoned with salt and pepper. Brown on all sides in cooking fat. Remove and set aside. Mix together bread cubes, salt and pepper, sage, onion, and butter. Put into a buttered 5-quart casserole or a small, covered roaster. Blend flour into pan drippings; add 1 cup of strained chicken broth and cream. Bring to boiling stirring constantly and cook 1 to 2 minutes. Add chicken from backs and necks to the dressing in the heatproof casserole. Pour thickened sauce over the meat and dressing and top with browned chicken pieces. Cover and bake at 350°F. 1 hour or until pieces are fork tender. *6 to 8 servings*

13TH PRESIDENT

1850-1853

Millard Fillmore was born on Jan. 7, 1800, in a log cabin in the village of Locke, Cayuga Co., New York, where his parents had moved two years previously from Bennington, Vt. Fillmore's ancestors, who for generations had been residents of New England, had not been distinguished either by wealth or by outstanding achievement.

In 1856, three years after leaving the White House, Fillmore ran, without success, for president on the American, or Know-Nothing, party ticket.

Almost every cookbook today contains some barbeque recipes, for the barbeque has literally moved indoors. Anyone with a fireplace can set in, or improvise, a small charcoal grill, and can enjoy the distinctive flavor of charcoal cooking the year around. Barbeques were popular with our presidents, too, especially our early Southern presidents. The first presidential barbeque we could find on record occurred in 1793. George Washington had journeyed south to lay the cornerstone of the new capitol-to-be. After appropriate ceremonies and the firing of artillery, Washington and the group repaired to a "booth," where a 500-pound oxen had been barbequed for the occasion. They're still roasting big steers in Texas, but most of us have to settle for something less than the whole hog or steer.

BARBEQUED CHICKEN, EVALYN I

2 cloves garlic, minced
1 tablespoon salt
2 heaping teaspoons dry mustard
1 teaspoon celery salt
1 teaspoon leaf thyme
   Pinch ground sage, nutmeg, marjoram
1 cup red wine vinegar
¾ cup dry vermouth
12 to 14 disjointed chicken pieces

Mix all ingredients, except chicken, in a large, shallow baking pan as a marinade. Place chicken in pan, skin side down, and marinate for 1 hour. Turn chicken in pan; marinate, refrigerated, for 4 to 6 hours. Reserve the marinade. When ready to barbeque, place chicken pieces on grill about 8 inches from coals. It takes about 30 to 40 min-

utes to grill using white hot coals. Turn occasionally. During the last half of cooking time, turn the chicken frequently and brush with the leftover marinade for flavor and crispness.

About 6 servings

Not everyone cares for the high seasonings of most barbeque recipes. Here is a bland, but exceptionally tenderizing, variation of chicken on the barbeque.

BARBEQUED CHICKEN, EVALYN II

2 small spring chickens
1 to 1½ cups sauterne
4 tablespoons butter
¼ teaspoon garlic salt
1 tablespoon chopped parsley
1 baster with steel injection needle

The combined weight of the young fryers should be about 5 to 5½ pounds. Halve and flatten the chickens. Your meat dealer will probably do this for you. Put the injection needle on the baster; these are obtainable at most hardware stores. Inject ½ cup or so of wine, depending on the size of the chicken, into the fleshy parts of the breasts and legs. Place pieces on grill and barbeque about 8 inches from hot charcoal, bone side down, for about 20 minutes. Turn chicken pieces and inject another ½ cup or so of wine into the fleshy part of the leg; drizzle some over the tops of the pieces also. Broil another 20 minutes, this time basting with the butter to which the garlic salt and parsley have been added.

4 servings

Rock Cornish game hen, the all-white meat bird developed for individual service, is a fairly new variety of poultry. It was unknown in President William Henry Harrison's day (1841). No doubt, though, that he would have loved it, as he loved game, and in his letters often mentioned spending time hunting grouse near his Indiana home. His estate, a handsome home today, but a real show-place in pioneer times, was named Grouseland, so abundant were the birds of that variety in the neighborhood. Unfortunately the most of us, the chances of obtaining grouse today are so unfavorable as to make a recipe of them impractical in this book. The quick-frozen Cornish game hen is easily found in any supermarket, and is an excellent choice for special dinners. The following recipe, with a forcemeat stuffing and cherry sauced, is named for the game-loving president who had the shortest term of office to date—one month.

William Henry Harrison's
CORNISH GAME HEN

- 4 Rock Cornish game hens, 16 to 18 ounces each
- 6 small pork sausage links
- 1 package frozen chicken livers
- ¼ pound butter, softened
- 1 tablespoon plus 1 teaspoon instant minced onion softened in an equal amount of water
- 1 teaspoon dry mustard
- ⅛ teaspoon ground mace
- ⅛ teaspoon ground cloves
- ⅛ teaspoon ground nutmeg
- Salt and pepper to taste
- Pat of unsalted butter
- Harrison Sauce (see recipe)

Bring the sausages and chicken livers to boiling together in water enough to cover; reduce heat and simmer for 20 minutes. Drain and put them through the finest blade of a food chopper. Make a paste of butter, minced onion, dry mustard, mace, cloves, and nutmeg. Mix well with the sausage-chicken liver paste and cool. Season inside the cavities of hens with salt and pepper. Loosely stuff the cavities with the forcemeat mixture. Pull loose skin over cavity openings; fasten with skewers. Fasten neck skin to back. Tie wings and legs to body. Brush hens with unsalted butter. Place, breast side up, in roasting pan and roast in a 400°F. oven about 1 hour. To serve, spoon on Harrison Sauce.

4 servings

Harrison Sauce

- 1 jar (17 ounces) pitted dark sweet cherries, drained and ¾ cup syrup reserved
- 1 cup canned beef gravy
- 2 tablespoons Madeira

Heat cherry syrup with canned beef gravy; add cherries and warm. Just before serving, add Madeira.　　*About 3 cups sauce*

Some historians give George Washington credit for the introduction of pheasants to the United States. Anyway, they are truly gourmet fare.

PHEASANTS WITH SPAETZLE

- 2 pheasants, cleaned and quartered
- 2 quarts boiling water
- 4 chicken bouillon cubes
- ½ cup flour
- 1 cup butter
- 1 teaspoon paprika
- 7 tablespoons flour
- 1 cup Chablis
- 1 cup dairy sour cream

Take necks, backs, giblets, et cetera from pheasants and simmer in water, strengthened with chicken bouillon cubes. Cook until stock is reduced to 1½ quarts. Flour remaining pieces of pheasant; saute in ½ cup butter until brown, and reserve. Melt remaining ½ cup butter in a large frying pan and add paprika. Strain pheasant stock and add all but 1 cup to butter and paprika. Bring to boiling. Adding gradually, stir a blend of about 1 cup cooled stock and the flour into stock. Boil 1 to 2 minutes. Stir in the Chablis and cook gently for 30 minutes. Then add browned pheasant; cover and cook until tender 1 to 1½ hours. Remove pheasant. Stir in sour cream, about a spoonful at a time. Heat but do not boil. Place pheasant in chafing or serving dish and spoon over some of the paprika sauce. Serve with spaetzle, also with paprika sauce spooned over them.　　*About 6 servings*

Spaetzle

Combine 3 beaten **eggs**, ½ teaspoon **salt**, and 1 cup **heavy cream**. Stir in **flour** (about 2 cups) to make a stiff batter. Drop from end of a teaspoon into some boiling **chicken stock**. Keep spaetzle no larger than a quarter by dipping enough to cover just the end of teaspoon. Cook 5 minutes and then drain. Saute in ¼ cup **butter** until light brown.

ROAST WILD DUCKS

3 wild ducks, about 2 pounds each
Salt
Raisin-Orange Stuffing (see recipe)
6 slices bacon, cut in halves
1 cup orange juice

Singe and clean ducks. Cut out oil sac at base of tail; cut off neck at body, leaving on neck skin. Wash ducks under cold running water; dry. Rub cavities with salt. Lightly stuff the cavities with Raisin-Orange Stuffing. Place ducks, breast side up, on rack in shallow roasting pan. Lay four bacon pieces over breast of each bird. Roast, uncovered, in a 450°F. oven 15 minutes for very rare, 20 minutes for medium rare, and 25 minutes for medium well. Baste ducks occasionally with orange juice during roasting. Place ducks on heated platter; reserve drippings for Orange Sauce (see recipe) to serve over ducks.

6 servings

Raisin-Orange Stuffing

6 cups ¼-inch bread cubes (slightly dry)
1 cup seedless raisins
½ cup butter
½ cup chopped onion
1 cup thinly sliced celery
1 tablespoon grated orange peel
1 teaspoon salt
½ teaspoon ground thyme
Few grains black pepper

Combine the bread cubes and raisins in a large bowl. Saute onion and celery in butter. Mix in orange peel and seasonings. Add to bread mixture and toss until well mixed. Spoon lightly into birds. *Stuffing for three 2-pound ducks*

Orange Sauce

2 tablespoons fat in roasting pan
3 tablespoons flour
½ cup water
⅔ cup orange juice
½ teaspoon grated orange peel
½ teaspoon grated lemon peel

Heat the fat in roasting pan. Add the flour and stir until smooth. Add the water gradually, stirring constantly. Continue to stir, bring to boiling, and cook 1 to 2 minutes. Blend in the orange juice and heat to boiling. Serve sauce topped with the grated peel. *About 1¼ cups sauce*

POTTED DUCK IN WINE SAUCE

4 to 5-pound duckling
2 cups Burgundy
¼ cup brandy
¼ cup undiluted frozen orange juice concentrate
1 onion, quartered
1 sprig parsley
¼ teaspoon ground thyme
½ teaspoon salt

Quarter duckling; put on a rack in a shallow baking pan. Roast in a 425°F. oven 30 minutes. Occasionally prick skin to let more fat run off. Pour off the drippings and remove rack from pan; place duck directly on the bottom; add remaining ingredients. Reduce oven heat to 350°F. and return to the oven. Cover and cook at least 2 hours or until duckling is tender. Serve with the pan gravy. If desired, thicken gravy with a blend of cornstarch and water; bring to boiling and cook 2 to 3 minutes, stirring constantly. *4 servings*

Franklin Pierce was born at Hillsboro, N.H., on Nov. 23, 1804. He received his education at several academies and at Bowdoin College in Maine. He studied law for three years, was admitted to the bar in 1827, and in 1829 was elected a member of the New Hampshire state legislature.

14TH PRESIDENT

1853-1857

The 1852 Democratic National Convention, after a long deadlock, accepted Pierce as a compromise "dark-horse" nominee because of his moderate views on the slavery issue.

John Adams, second President and first occupant of the newly built White House, ordered the Sevres china set of which this elegant tureen was a part.

President Madison's orange and black French Nast porcelain survived the British burning of the White House in 1814.

Three pieces from Andrew Jackson's Biennais service are on the hunt board in the President's second floor dining room.

THE
Presidents'
CHINA
COLLECTION

Traditionally, our Presidents and First Ladies have selected the state china used in the White House during each administration. These examples help illustrate the continuity of formal hospitality in the President's House.

This French porcelain fish platter exemplifies the colorful design of John Quincy Adams' state china.

A surprisingly delicate floral design selected by the soldier-President, Ulysses S. Grant.

Created by Dagoty in France for James Monroe: amaranthine border with ornamental medallions.

Grey-gold and white Spode used at the White House wedding of President Van Buren's son.

President James K. Polk and his gracious First Lady approved this service for a temperance White House.

The simple, red bordered saucer, butter pat, and platter seem to reflect the subdued ways of President Franklin Pierce and the invalid Mrs. Pierce.

American flora and fauna were depicted on the 1000-piece Haviland china of Rutherford B. Hayes.

President and Mrs. Garfield moved their family china to the White House with them in 1881.

The Lincolns' French porcelain service by Haviland: (left) plate, compote, platter; (right) double-handled custard cup and plate.

Benjamin Harrison ordered this Limoges china with its border of corn and goldenrod. It was used during the second administration of Grover Cleveland.

Top L — The seal of the United States and
border design in flat gold
distinguished the state china of Theodore Roosevelt.

Top R — Lenox china service plate of set purchased during
the administration of Woodrow Wilson.

Lower L — Green and gold state service by Lenox used
during the Truman and Eisenhower administrations.

Lower R — During more than 12 years of depression,
recovery, and war the Franklin D. Roosevelts
used President James Monroe's gold service
and this blue-and-gold bordered Lenox.

LEFT — Gold trimmed service plate from
Dwight D. Eisenhower's state service by Castleton.

Duck hunting was George Washington's favorite sport. Another president who dearly loved hunting and fishing was Grover Cleveland. The following is his recipe for Braised Ducks.

Grover Cleveland's
BRAISED DUCKS

2 3-pound Mallard ducks
3 slices bacon
1 large carrot
1 medium onion
2 whole cloves
1 sprig parsley
¼ teaspoon ground thyme
¼ teaspoon pepper
1 pint chicken stock
½ cup white wine
1½ pounds white turnips
¼ cup butter
2 tablespoons cornstarch
¼ cup cold water

Prepare a pair of fine young ducks, the same as for roasting, place them in a stew pan together with 2 or 3 slices of bacon, a carrot, and onion stuck with 2 cloves, and a little parsley and thyme. Season with pepper and cover the whole with a broth, adding to the broth a gill of white wine (8 tablespoons). Place the pan, covered, over low heat and allow the ducks to simmer until done, basting them frequently. When ducks are done, remove from pan, and place them where they will keep hot. Turnips should then be pared, cut up and fried in some butter. When nicely browned, drain the pieces and cook them until tender in the liquid in which the ducks were braised; reserve turnip pieces. Now strain and thicken the gravy, and after dishing up the ducks, pour it over them, garnishing with the pieces of turnip. To thicken gravy, blend the cornstarch with the water. Stir into boiling gravy. Cook 2 to 3 minutes, continuing to stir.

About 6 servings

Foods
From The Sea

THE ORIGINAL UNITED STATES hugged the shore of the Atlantic Ocean which had been the colonists' stormy path from Europe, the route of early American trade, and a bountiful source of the fish and seafood which have been a flavorsome and important part of our diet ever since. The new country slowly expanded westward until the great Pacific added its variety of maritime delicacies to the national cuisine.

Here, then, are authentic recipes for eighteen delectable dishes frequently served at the White House. They feature fish from the sea and brook trout fresh-caught by President Eisenhower, as well as clams, crab meat, scallops, shrimp, smelts and finnan haddie.

James Buchanan

James Buchanan was born on Apr. 23, 1791, in a one-room log cabin at Stony Batter, near Mercersburg, Pa. After graduation in 1809, from Dickinson College, Carlisle, Pa., he studied law for three years and was admitted to the bar in 1812.

15TH PRESIDENT

1857-1861

President Buchanan was host at the White House in May, 1860, to the first Japanese delegation to come to the U.S. The visit of the Japanese ministers, with their entourage of 60 persons, helped to cement the "open-door" relations between Japan and the nations of the Western world.

This is a simple but appealing way to serve almost any fish fillet or steak. We suggest halibut, swordfish, or salmon steaks. But fillet of whitefish, haddock, cod, bass, bluefish, pompano, snapper, or flounder are equally good.

BAKED FISH FILLETS

8 **fish fillets or steaks**
  Butter
  Salt
  Milk

Olive-Pimiento Sauce

1 **tablespoon butter**
½ **cup sliced mushrooms**
¼ **cup butter**
4 **tablespoons flour**
3 **cups chicken stock**
  Pinch dry mustard
1 **teaspoon onion juice**
  Pimiento strips, drained (reserve 1 teaspoon liquid)
¼ **teaspoon Worcestershire sauce**
  Salt to taste
¼ **cup sliced, pitted ripe olives**

Rub fillets with butter and season lightly with salt. Place in a greased shallow casserole and add enough milk to cover fish. Bake at 325°F. 45 minutes, or until fish flakes easily. Drain and discard milk. While fish is baking prepare the sauce. Saute mushrooms a few minutes in 1 tablespoon butter. Remove mushrooms with a slotted spoon and reserve. Melt ¼ cup butter in a saucepan over low heat; stir in the flour to make a **roux.** Stirring constantly, slowly add chicken stock (may be made with chicken bouillon cubes to which a dash of dry mustard has been added). Bring to boiling; cook and stir until sauce is thick and smooth. Mix in the reserved mushrooms and remaining ingredients. Pour hot sauce over fish. *8 servings*

When Mrs. Roosevelt (FDR) went to the White House, her old family cookbook was alongside Mrs. Nesbitt's in her housekeeping office. Mrs. Roosevelt was frank to admit that she had not done much cooking during her life. But one of the dishes she did serve her family was Kedgeree, a simple English dish. A teaspoon of onion juice, a teaspoon of Worcestershire sauce, and a tablespoon of curry powder added to this dish when she calls for "seasoning to taste" helps a lot.

Eleanor Roosevelt's
ENGLISH KEDGEREE

Mix together 1 cup **boiled white fish** (flaked), 1 cup **boiled rice,** 2 **hard-cooked eggs,** and **seasoning** to taste. Put in oven to brown. Serve hot. The hard-cooked eggs, are, of course, chopped and added. If one likes the mixture a little moist, milk may be added. It is good served with a hot tomato or chili sauce, or pepper pot.

2 to 4 servings

Former President Eisenhower was a golfer of some stature, and well known for his love of the game. But golf was not his only sport. Two other favorites were quail hunting and trout fishing. And when it comes to fish cookery, nothing can beat this recipe as Eisenhower meant it to be. That is, a freshly caught, cold brook trout pulled from the stream, then promptly cleaned and cooked alongside it. Not all of us can be this fortunate in preparing trout this way, but you can approximate his "Open-Fire Trout" by doing it on the outdoor grill.

President Eisenhower's
OPEN-FIRE TROUT

6 brook trout (¾ pound each)
Olive oil
Pepper to taste
½ cup cornmeal

Clean trout, dip in olive oil, season with pepper, and coat with cornmeal. Wrap each fish in aluminum foil and cook on the grill 10 minutes to each side. Charcoal should be at the peak of its heat—still glowing after the flames have died.

6 servings

Smelts were originally ocean fish and when they ran into the tidewaters to spawn, they were often caught and served on the menus at Mt. Vernon, George Washington's home. Then smelts were introduced into the Great Lakes. In early spring they make their run into shallow waters to spawn. Lucky fishermen fish by light at night and dip nets into the shallow water to bring up the little silver delicacies by the pailful.

PAN-FRIED SMELTS

2 pounds smelts, cleaned
½ cup cornmeal or flour
1 teaspoon salt
¼ teaspoon pepper
1 egg, beaten slightly with 1 tablespoon water
Fine, dry bread crumbs
Butter (or fat for deep frying, heated to 375°F.)

Wipe smelts with a damp cloth, then coat with cornmeal or flour seasoned with salt and pepper. Dip fish in egg, then coat well with fine crumbs. Let rest 5 minutes. Fry in butter until browned on each side, or deep fry in hot fat until just golden brown.

2 to 4 servings

President Kennedy was guest of honor at a dinner at McCormick Place, April 28, 1961, during his first post-election visit to Chicago. The banquet menu served was: Fresh fruit in a pineapple basket, salted nuts, celery hearts, rose-bud radishes, ripe and green olives, cream of mushroom soup, filet of boneless Dover sole with lobster filling and Veronique sauce; tiny parsleyed potatoes, fresh asparagus in browned butter, and limestone lettuce and tomato salad with vinaigrette dressing. The specially created desserts of ice cream bombes were called "New Frontier" and served, en parade, by the waiters. The ice cream was topped with Pilgrim rum sauce; assorted cookies and coffee followed. The following is the recipe for the entree, filet of boneless Dover sole, adapted for home cooking. The secret to the out-of-this-world taste of this dish is in using fresh Dover or Boston sole.

John F. Kennedy's
STUFFED DOVER SOLE

2 Dover sole (1 pound each)
¾ cup lobster meat, finely diced
¼ cup finely diced mushrooms
2 tablespoons minced shallot*
4 tablespoons butter
2 tablespoons dry white wine
Salt to taste
Dash Tabasco
2 eggs, beaten
Baking parchment
Veronique Sauce (page 82)

Bone and remove skin from the sole. Make a lobster **farce** (filling) as follows: saute mushrooms and shallot in butter; add lobster meat, wine, salt, and Tabasco. Mix well; stir in eggs slowly over low heat. Cook, stirring until farce is thickened. Cool. Place an ounce or so of lobster filling on each fillet of sole and fold fish over from each end, envelope style, to cover. Put fillets on a buttered baking sheet; cover with well-greased parchment. Bake in a 375°-400°F. oven 30 to 40 minutes, or until fish flakes easily. Before serving, top with Veronique Sauce.

4 servings

*If shallot is unobtainable, substitute a thin clove of garlic and a green onion, both finely minced.

BUFFET SEAFOOD SUPREME

- ¾ cup butter
- ¾ cup flour
- 3 cups milk
- 1½ cups Gruyère cheese (in small pieces)
- ⅛ teaspoon garlic powder
- ⅛ teaspoon white pepper
- ¼ teaspoon dry mustard
- 1 teaspoon salt
- 1 tablespoon tomato paste
- 1 tablespoon lemon juice
- ½ cup bottled clam juice
- ¼ pound sliced mushrooms
- ¼ cup butter
- 1 pound cooked shrimp
- 1 package (6 ounces) frozen Alaska king crab
- 1 pound cooked lobster meat
- ¼ cup diced green pepper

Melt ¾ cup butter in a heavy saucepan over medium heat; blend in the flour and cook until bubbly. Stir in the milk and cook, stirring constantly, until sauce comes to boiling and is thickened and smooth. Add the cheese; cook and stir until cheese is melted. Add a mixture of the garlic powder and next 3 ingredients, then the tomato paste and next 2 ingredients. Blend thoroughly. Saute mushrooms in ¼ cup butter; add

mushrooms to the sauce and reserve the mushroom butter. Add cooked shrimp, and crab and lobster meat, separate in pieces. Heat thoroughly. Meanwhile, saute green pepper until tender in reserved mushroom butter. Serve the seafood garnished with the green pepper over hot **rice.** *8 servings*

President Kennedy's
BAKED SEAFOOD CASSEROLE

- ½ pound fresh, cooked crab meat
- ½ pound fresh, cooked lobster meat
- 1 pound cooked, deveined shrimp
- 1 cup mayonnaise
- ½ cup chopped green pepper
- ¼ cup chopped green onion
- 1½ cups chopped celery
- ½ teaspoon salt
- 1 tablespoon Worcestershire sauce
- 2 cups crushed potato chips

Mix all ingredients except potato chips and turn into a greased casserole. Cover with the crushed potato chips. Sprinkle with **paprika.** Heat in a 400°F. oven 20 to 25 minutes.

6 to 8 servings

Abraham Lincoln was born in a log cabin in Hardin Co., Kentucky, on Feb. 12, 1809, to Thomas and Nancy Hanks Lincoln. He lived in Kentucky until 1816 when the Lincoln family moved to Indiana.

16TH PRESIDENT

1861-1865

Lincoln's address at the dedication of the soldiers cemetery at Gettysburg, on Nov. 19, 1863, revealed his passionate belief in the endurance of popular government.

The gay mood of the Fourth of July holiday, 1876, was captured in a commemorative painting, "The Day We Celebrate" by F. A. Chapman, painted for the centenary of Independence, which was observed when Ulysses S. Grant was president.

Delmonico is a dish to serve people who are not sure they will like fish. Serve it accompanied by fluffy rice, in baked patty shells, on English muffins, or toast points. It's a rich, elegant dish, also worthy of chafing dish service.

FINNAN HADDIE DELMONICO

1½ pounds finnan haddie
1 pound cooked shrimp, diced
¼ cup butter

Rich Cream Sauce
1 cup butter
2 tablespoons flour
1 cup milk
½ cup light cream
3 egg yolks, beaten

4 hard-cooked eggs, diced
Salt and white pepper
Yellow food coloring (optional)

Soak finnan haddie in water 2 hours; drain and reserve water. Cut finnan haddie into ½-ounce cubes. Heat reserved water to boiling; add fish and poach gently about 15 minutes. Drain and flake fish. Melt butter in a saucepan; add the haddie and shrimp and gently saute about 5 minutes. Meanwhile, prepare the cream sauce. In a heavy saucepan melt the butter over low heat; stir in the flour. Blend in the milk and cream, a little at a time; cook slowly, stirring until slightly thickened and smooth. Stir some of the hot sauce into egg yolks; blend well and return mixture to saucepan. Cook and stir over low heat until sauce is thick and smooth (do not boil). Add cream sauce to the fish mixture. Cover and simmer gently a few minutes. Add eggs and season to taste with salt and white pepper. Add a drop of food coloring, if needed.

6 to 8 servings

BROOK TROUT AMANDINE

6 brook trout (¾ pound each)
Salad oil
¼ cup butter
½ cup slivered blanched almonds
6 slices cooked bacon
Lemon wedges

Wash trout, pat dry, and brush lightly with oil. Broil several inches from the heat, turning once, 5 to 7 minutes on each side. Saute the almonds in butter. Place the trout on a heated platter and pour the "foaming" butter with almonds over them. Top each fish with a slice of crisp bacon and serve garnished with lemon wedges.

6 servings

Presidential clambakes were in vogue when Chester Alan Arthur was president, back in the early 1880's. Arthur was a handsome widower, a gourmet, and the darling of the elite of Newport society. He enjoyed travel, and often went to Rhode Island to be entertained with a traditional New England clambake. The oceanside pits were filled with fiery hot stones, lobsters, and clams. The clams and lobsters were cooked, blanketed by seaweed. Once the province of the coastlines, clambakes now are enjoyed anywhere in the country. Eastern fish houses will fly the live lobsters to you, also the clams, the necessary seaweed, and even the kettle and cooking instructions. But the best way to enjoy an inland clambake is to purchase a 3-tiered clam steamer, available in better department stores and specialty shops in metropolitan areas. The spigot on the bottom of the steamer is used to draw off steaming, delicious clam broth, a wonderful starter course.

MIDWESTERN CLAMBAKE

- 8 small onions
- 8 small white potatoes, pared
- 8 small carrots, scraped
- 8 small pork sausage links
- 1 package cheesecloth
- ½ peck soft-shell clams
- Seaweed (comes with clams)
- 1 clam steamer
- 4 quarts water
- 2 bottles (8 ounces each) clam juice
- 8 live Maine lobsters (1¾ pounds each)

To be done ahead of time: Cut cheesecloth into 8 squares. On each piece of cheesecloth place 1 onion, 1 potato, 1 carrot, and 1 sausage. Tie ends to form a little bag. Then scrub and scrub the clams. They are very sandy and must be thoroughly washed or you will end up with gritty clam broth instead of a nectar of the gods. Also wash seaweed. One more word of caution; lobsters should be added to the steamer WHILE ALIVE. Add 4 quarts water and the bottled clam juice to the bottom section of the steamer. Place on a rack or grill, out-of-doors, over a hot, wood fire. Bring liquids to a rolling boil. (It's easier to use a roaring wood fire than charcoal because high heat must be maintained to steam the seafood.) In the first steamer above the bottom spigotted one, place the filled cheesecloth bags, then the clams. In the top, or third, section place the lobsters covered by the washed seaweed. Steam over high heat 1 hour. Then reverse the position of the clam section and lobster section and steam

1 hour longer. Test for doneness. A raw potato put on top of the top section is a good way to test for doneness. The lobsters will be red, the vegetables soft, and the clams opened.   *8 servings*

An equally delicious clambake, using the special clam steamer, is made with chicken instead of lobsters. . . . particularly good in sweet corn season!

CLAMBAKE WITH CHICKEN

- 4 broiler-fryer chickens (2½ pounds each)
- ½ pound butter, softened
- 1 teaspoon chopped chives
- 1 teaspoon chopped parsley
- Salt
- Onion salt
- Garlic salt
- 12 small sweet potatoes, scrubbed and parboiled 20 minutes
- 24 ears fresh sweet corn, husked
- 1 peck clams and seaweed
- 4 quarts water
- 2 bottles (8 ounces each) clam juice
- Drawn butter

To be done ahead of time: have the butcher flatten and quarter the chickens. Make an herb butter by adding chives, parsley, salt, onion salt, and garlic salt to butter. Chicken will be too bland without plenty of seasoned salt. With a paring knife, gently lift chicken skin away from the meat. Generously butter chicken in those pockets, wherever possible; then roll back the skin to cover again. Wash seaweed and thoroughly scrub the clams free from sand. Add the water and the clam juice to the bottom section of the steamer. Place on a rack or grill, out-of-doors, over a hot, wood fire. Bring liquid to a rolling boil. In the first steamer above the bottom spigotted section layer the chicken pieces, then the partially cooked sweet potatoes, and the ears of corn. A few celery leaves will give added flavor. In the top section of the steamer, place the clams and washed seaweed. Steam over a hot fire 1 hour and 15 minutes to 2 hours. A good way to test for doneness is to put an extra sweet potato at the very top, on top of the clams and seaweed. When that potato is tender, everything in steamer should be done. Draw off the clam broth and serve as a first course; then serve clams with extra broth and plenty of drawn butter. Next come the chicken, corn, and sweet potatoes.   *12 servings*

Since this "salad" is a main dish, and a delightful luncheon one, rather than an accompaniment, we include it among seafood, rather than the chapter featuring salads.

HOT CRAB MEAT SALAD

½ cup butter
⅔ cup flour
2⅔ cups milk
3 packages (6 ounces each) frozen
   Alaska king crab meat
2 cups diced celery
½ cup minced green pepper
¼ cup minced pimiento
⅓ cup slivered almonds
2 teaspoons salt
   Herb-seasoned stuffing mix
   Butter
   Lettuce cups

Melt butter in a medium saucepan; stir in the flour. Add milk gradually, cooking and stirring until sauce is thickened and smooth. Add the crab meat and the next 5 ingredients; mix well. Turn into a buttered 2-quart casserole. Crush some herb-seasoned stuffing mix until it is as fine as bread crumbs. Sprinkle over the top of casserole and dot with bits of butter. Bake in a 325°F. oven about 35 minutes. Serve hot spooning into fresh crisp lettuce cups.

6 to 8 servings

Lobster Newburg—a great favorite of President Taft—was a most popular turn-of-the-century dish. *A famous New York restaurateur named it after one of his favorite customers, a gentleman named Wenburg. When Wenburg and the proprietor had a falling out, the proprietor took his revenge by reversing the spelling of the name... or so the story goes.*

LOBSTER NEWBURG

½ cup sliced fresh mushrooms
2 tablespoons butter
1 pound cooked lobster pieces
2 tablespoons butter
½ cup Madeira
2 tablespoons brandy
1½ cups heavy cream, scalded
3 egg yolks, beaten
   Dash of ground mace
   Salt

Saute mushrooms in 2 tablespoons butter and reserve. Gently heat lobster in remaining butter with the wine, cooking until the wine is reduced by half. Add brandy and set aflame. When flame has died down, put the mixture into the top of a double boiler over low heat. Add mushrooms and cream; mix well. Stir a little of the hot sauce into the egg yolks; return to mixture in double boiler. Cook over simmering water until sauce is thickened, stirring frequently. Add mace and salt to taste. Serve at once spooned into pastry shells.

About 6 servings

NOTE: Lobster Newburg is a dish that adapts itself well to chafing dish cookery. Crab may be interchanged with the lobster meat.

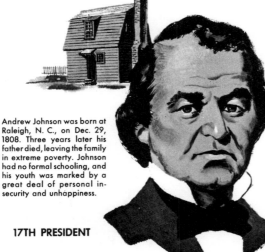

Andrew Johnson was born at Raleigh, N. C., on Dec. 29, 1808. Three years later his father died, leaving the family in extreme poverty. Johnson had no formal schooling, and his youth was marked by a great deal of personal insecurity and unhappiness.

17TH PRESIDENT

1865-1869

Carpetbaggers plagued the South in Reconstruction days as Johnson, who became President upon Lincoln's death, toured the region on a speech-making tour in 1866 in a gesture of reconciliation.

601 North County Road, Palm Beach, Florida, received much attention as the location of the "Winter White House" during the Kennedy administration. One of the popular dinner menus of the president while there was Florida Stone Crabs followed by Pompano. Both were flown, on occasion, to the White House in Washington. Florida stone crabs are prepared much the same as live lobster. Unfortunately for most of the country, stone crabs are highly perishable and, therefore, are not generally available outside Florida. Only the large claw of the crab is used. These are boiled, chilled, then eaten cold, dipped in drawn butter or a special sauce. Following is the special sauce that was favored by President Kennedy ... if you're lucky enough to be preparing Florida stone crabs.

FLORIDA STONE CRABS A LA KENNEDY

      1 crab claw per serving
        Boiling salted water
      1 tablespoon cooking oil
      1 tablespoon lime juice

Special Dipping Sauce

     10 tablespoons mayonnaise
      4 tablespoons steak sauce
      7 tablespoons golden prepared mustard
     10 drops Tabasco
        Juice of 1 lemon

Add oil and lime juice to boiling salted water. Drop in the stone crab claws and cook until tender. Remove from water and chill. To prepare the sauce, mix the ingredients thoroughly in a prechilled bowl. Before serving claws crack the shells in many places so the meat can be easily removed. Dip crab pieces into sauce and eat.

1⅓ cups sauce

Shrimp de Jonghe is named after its creator, a late Chicago restaurateur.

SHRIMP DE JONGHE

      2 pounds raw shrimp
      1 tablespoon pickling spices
      1 tablespoon lemon juice
      ¼ pound butter, softened
      2 cloves garlic, crushed
      ¾ cup herb-seasoned stuffing mix,
        finely crushed
      2 tablespoons chopped parsley
      ¼ cup dry sherry

Shell and devein raw shrimp. Add spices and lemon juice to 1 quart rapidly boiling water. Add

shrimp and reduce heat to simmer; cook 3 to 5 minutes. Drain shrimp. Blend garlic into the butter, then work in the crushed herb-seasoned stuffing, parsley, and sherry. Arrange shrimp in buttered individual ramekins or in 6-inch scallop shells; top with the seasoned mixture. Place in a 400°F. oven 10 to 15 minutes.   *4 servings*

This is a very satisfactory luncheon or late supper dish and simple to prepare.

SHRIMP BAKED IN MADEIRA

      1 pound frozen deveined shrimp
      1 teaspoon pickling spices
      1 tablespoon lemon juice
        Few celery leaves
      1 cup sliced fresh mushrooms
      4 tablespoons butter
      2 tablespoons flour
      ½ cup cream
      2 tablespoons Madeira
      2 ripe avocados
        Salt to taste
      ¼ cup herb-seasoned stuffing
        mix, finely crushed

Cook shrimp about 4 minutes in 1 quart of boiling, salted water with pickling spices, lemon juice, and a few celery leaves. Drain shrimp (do not overcook or shrimp will become rubbery). Saute mushrooms in 2 tablespoons of butter. Melt remaining butter in a saucepan. Mix in the flour and heat until bubbly. Gradually add the cream, stirring constantly; bring to boiling and cook 1 to 2 minutes. Remove from heat; add the mushrooms and 2 tablespoons Madeira. Cut avocados into halves and remove pits and skin; lightly salt them. Place avocado halves in individual ramekins, or close together in a shallow baking dish. Add shrimp to Madeira sauce and spoon shrimp mixture over avocados. Sprinkle the crushed stuffing mix over the top. Heat in a 300°F. oven 15 minutes.   *4 servings*

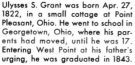

Ulysses S. Grant was born Apr. 27, 1822, in a small cottage at Point Pleasant, Ohio. He went to school in Georgetown, Ohio, where his parents had moved, until he was 17. Entering West Point at his father's urging, he was graduated in 1843.

18TH PRESIDENT

1869-1877

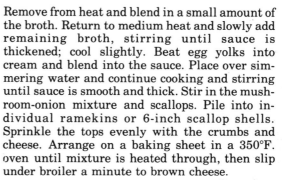

On Apr. 9, 1865, Lee surrendered the army of Northern Virginia to Grant, now chief of Union forces, at Appomattox Court House.

COQUILLES ST. JACQUES

- 1 cup dry white wine
- 2 tablespoons butter
- 2 tablespoons chopped parsley
  Pinch of thyme
- 1 bay leaf
- 2 pounds scallops, washed and drained
- 2 tablespoons butter
- 2 cups chopped fresh mushrooms
- 6 green onions, chopped
- ⅓ cup water
  Juice of 1 lemon
- ½ teaspoon salt
  Few grains cayenne pepper
- 3 tablespoons butter
- 2 tablespoons flour
- 4 egg yolks
- 1 cup heavy cream
  Buttered herb-seasoned stuffing mix, finely crushed
- 2 tablespoons shredded Parmesan cheese

Combine the first 5 ingredients in a shallow pan or large skillet; bring quickly to boiling. Add scallops; reduce heat to simmer and poach scallops 5 minutes. Remove scallops from pan; strain and reserve the broth. Finely chop the scallops and set aside. Melt 2 tablespoons butter; add mushrooms and onion and saute 3 minutes, or until soft. Add water and next 3 ingredients. Cook 3 minutes longer. Drain and set aside mushrooms and onion; add the liquid to strained wine broth. Melt 3 tablespoons butter in top of a double boiler over direct heat; stir in the flour.

Remove from heat and blend in a small amount of the broth. Return to medium heat and slowly add remaining broth, stirring until sauce is thickened; cool slightly. Beat egg yolks into cream and blend into the sauce. Place over simmering water and continue cooking and stirring until sauce is smooth and thick. Stir in the mushroom-onion mixture and scallops. Pile into individual ramekins or 6-inch scallop shells. Sprinkle the tops evenly with the crumbs and cheese. Arrange on a baking sheet in a 350°F. oven until mixture is heated through, then slip under broiler a minute to brown cheese.

8 servings

DEEP-FRIED FAN TAILED SHRIMP

- 24 shrimps (tails left on and shrimp cleaned and split halfway through their length)
- 2 eggs, slightly beaten
- 1 tablespoon water
- 1 cup corn flake crumbs
- 1 teaspoon salt
  Pinch white pepper (optional)
  Fat for deep frying, heated to 375°F.

Combine eggs and water. Combine corn flake crumbs, salt, and pepper, if used. Dip shrimp into egg, then coat well with crumbs. Let rest 10 minutes. Fry shrimp in hot fat until golden brown. (Take care not to overcook shrimp; this makes them stringy and rubbery.) Drain shrimp on absorbent paper. Serve with **tartar sauce** or **chili sauce.**

4 to 6 servings

"Pic Nick, Camden, Maine" is a typical scene during the 1850's, about the time that Franklin Pierce took office, when city dwellers enjoyed relaxation in the outdoors with friends and neighbors during their few leisure hours.

Vegetables

. . . from Jefferson's garden to Kennedy's kitchen

Fresh vegetables? Practically unheard of in colonial America. The early presidents . . . Washington, Jefferson, Madison, Monroe . . . were the notable exceptions. They all had greenhouses; grew such exotic (then) vegetables as broccoli and artichokes; raised oranges and lemons, all under glass. It never occurred to the average colonial to put in a vegetable garden. The Indians had taught him to eat succotash (a dish originating with them). And the colonial dried turnips and pumpkins and beans for winter use. His fresh vegetables remained the wild spring greens plucked from the countryside—cowslip, dandelions, fiddleheads (ferns), milkweed leaves, et cetera. Abigail Adams, wife of our second president, wrote that there were times during the Revolution that the Adamses had only greens and salt pork upon which to subsist. Tomatoes were called "love apples" and were grown strictly for decorative purposes. Until the middle of the 19th century, tomatoes were thought to be poisonous, being a member of the deadly nightshade family. In the enjoyment of vegetable dishes, the presidents fared somewhat better than the public. John Quincy Adams became interested in horticulture while a resident of the White House. He was the first to plant gardens and trees, and to landscape the grounds of the mansion. For the next forty years, the chief executive's fresh vegetables were supplied from his own White House kitchen garden, located on the east side of the mansion. During President Andrew Johnson's term, he had the out buildings of the east side backyard torn down and grass planted in place of the gardens.

Thomas Jefferson was our president most interested in the cultivation and preparation of vegetables for the table. The Jefferson cookbook, now in the White House China Room, contains the following "receipts" penned in Jefferson's own hand:

TO DRESS POTATOES — Wash your **potatoes** well and pare them. Let them lay 15 minutes in cold water. Take them out and throw them into as much boiling water and salt as will boil them tender soft. When done take them out of the water and mash them with a spoon; add **cream** and **butter** equal quantities, enough to make them liquid, with a little **nutmeg.** Stir them until perfectly light and white. If too stiff they may be liquified with good **milk.**

CHINESE MODE OF BOILING RICE — Wash **rice** well in cold water. When pulpy take it with a ladle; put it in a clean vessel. Let it remain (near the fire) till it becomes white and dry. In this form it is used for bread.

JEFFERSON'S DRIED BEANS — Boil **dried beans** till done but not mashed. Take a bit of **butter** the size of a walnut, ½ an **onion,** chopped fine. Do them together in a frying pan till the onion is done. Dash in a little **flour** and **broth** enough to make a gravy. Put in your beans, let them boil and season with **pepper** and **salt.**

CABBAGE PUDDING — Shred ½ pound of **lean beef** and a pound of **suet** very fine, add the **yolks of 3 eggs,** 1 spoonful **grated bread,** some **sweet herbs, pepper, salt,** and **onion.** It will fill a **cabbage** which must be parboiled and opened at the top. Scoop it out till you think it will receive the meat. Fill it, close it up, tie it hard, and close in a cloth. When it has boiled a little, tie it closer. It must boil 2½ hours.

SAUTEED ARTICHOKE ROUNDS, PARMESAN

    8 artichoke rounds (bottoms)
    4 tablespoons butter
       Salt to taste
       Lemon juice
       Grated Parmesan cheese

If you are using fresh artichokes to get the rounds, prepare them as for steamed artichokes, this page. Remove leaves and choke and you will have the rounds or bottoms. If you are using canned artichoke bottoms, you'll find them fairly expensive, but just as good as the fresh ones, and uniform in size. Melt butter in saucepan or skillet, and when it foams, saute artichokes quickly, while butter is darkening to a light brown. Sprinkle in some salt and a tablespoon of lemon juice. Sprinkle each top with grated Parmesan cheese. Place under a broiler with tops about 3 inches from source of heat. Broil about 2 minutes, or until cheese bubbles and the edges brown.

4 servings

The early rich colonials of Virginia grew and enjoyed globe artichokes. Before that, the Spanish had introduced artichokes into what is now California. But it took many years, mostly since the second World War, for artichokes to become popular the country over. They are served cold in appetizers or salads (see George Washington Salad). Served hot, they are a delicious steamed vegetable with a delicate nutty flavor.

ARTICHOKES, STEAMED WHOLE

    4 globe artichokes
    1 tablespoon salad oil
    1 tablespoon lemon juice
       Drawn butter

Rinse artichokes well, cut off ½ inch of the tops with a knife. Pull off tough or discolored leaves around artichoke bottom; cut off stem. With kitchen scissors, snip off the prickly end of each leaf. Place artichokes, upright, in deep covered kettle in 2 inches of boiling, salted water. Add salad oil, lemon juice; cover and steam until done, 25 to 45 minutes, depending on the size of the globe artichoke. The vegetable is done when the leaves pull out easily. Invert artichoke to drain. Serve, accompanied by drawn butter, or lemon butter. Pull out leaves, one by one, and eat the white bottom part of the leaf, after dipping it in the butter. When leaves have all been discarded, carefully cut out the prickly choke, eating the delicious bottom or round, also dipped in butter.

4 servings

In the White House during the Kennedy occupancy, asparagus was often served with its classic French sauce, Maltaise Sauce, said to be the finest sauce for asparagus.

MALTAISE SAUCE FOR ASPARAGUS

Make a **Hollandaise sauce** and add to it ½ teaspoon **grated orange peel** and the juice of 2 **blood oranges** (if you can find them). Serve over asparagus spears.

Eye appeal is important to this recipe. It is easier to buy the extra large, fancy asparagus in jars, as they are uniform in size and color. Cold Asparagus Chantilly is a nice complement to a luncheon of cheese soufflé and a quick bread; it can be arranged on platters for buffets with a sauceboat of Chantilly Cream alongside.

COLD ASPARAGUS CHANTILLY

- **1 jar (12 ounces) fancy green asparagus spears**
- **¼ cup whipped cream**
- **¼ cup mayonnaise**
- **¼ teaspoon vanilla extract**

Place the jar of asparagus spears in the refrigerator until well chilled. Allow 3 fancy spears per serving. Arrange spears on plate and top with Chantilly Cream: whip cream, fold in mayonnaise and flavor with vanilla extract.

4 servings

The garnish Polonaise means to accompany with bread crumbs that have been lightly browned in butter. For a slightly subtle variation, try finely crushed herb-seasoned stuffing mix in place of the bread crumbs. Flowerets of broccoli and cauliflower can be substituted for the asparagus.

ASPARAGUS POLONAISE

- **2 pounds fresh asparagus**
- **2 tablespoons herb-seasoned stuffing mix, finely crushed**
- **⅓ cup butter**
- **Few drops of lemon juice**

Allow ½ pound of fresh asparagus per serving.

Cut off white or pithy end of asparagus; cook in water or steam until done. Keep warm while whipping together this easy Polonaise Sauce: brown butter lightly in a saucepan; when the right color, add the crushed stuffing mix and brown lightly. Sprinkle with a few drops of lemon juice; pour over asparagus spears. (Finely chopped hard-cooked eggs are sometimes sprinkled over Asparagus Polonaise.)

4 servings

A good vegetable garnish with baked beans is banana fritters. As a supper or brunch dish, they go well with bacon or Canadian bacon.

BANANA FRITTERS, IRENE

- **1 cup all-purpose flour**
- **2 teaspoons baking powder**
- **3 tablespoons sugar**
- **¼ teaspoon salt**
- **1 egg, well beaten**
- **¼ cup milk**
- **1 tablespoon lemon juice**
- **3 firm ripe bananas with all-yellow peel**
- **Oil for deep frying, heated to 375°F.**

These fritters take about 5 minutes to prepare and about 5 minutes per panful to cook. Sift together the flour, baking powder, sugar, and salt. Beat 1 egg very light; add the milk; then stir slowly into the dry ingredients, stirring and beating until batter is smooth. Add lemon juice; beat again. Mash and rub 3 bananas through a sieve and beat the pulp into the batter. Drop by rounded tablespoonfuls into hot fat and fry until golden brown, turning to brown evenly.

About 1½ dozen fritters

Rutherford B. Hayes was born at Delaware, Ohio, on Oct. 4, 1822, shortly after the death of his farmer father. He studied at a New England academy, Kenyon College in Ohio, and Harvard Law School, where he stayed for a year and a half. He was admitted to the Ohio bar in 1845

19TH PRESIDENT

1877-1881

The Hayes-Tilden disputed presidential election of 1876 hung on contested returns from four Southern states, finally resulted in victory for Hayes, who received 185 electoral votes to Tilden's 184.

A President from Massachusetts ought to have a liking for the famous Boston baked beans, so here is the recipe from the Kennedy clan. Almost all Kennedy family recipes are large, as is the family, and more apt to serve a couple of dozen than the average recipe of 6 portions. The Kennedy bean recipe is reminiscent of Maine's famous "bean hole" beans.

Mrs. Kennedy's
BOSTON BAKED BEANS

1 pound navy (pea) beans
½ small onion, chopped
⅛ pound salt pork, diced
6 tablespoons brown sugar or molasses
¼ cup catsup
½ teaspoon dry mustard
1 teaspoon salt
1½ teaspoons Worcestershire sauce
2 cups boiling water
⅛ pound salt pork, cut in strips

Cover beans and soak overnight. Drain, cover with fresh water, and simmer slowly. When skins burst when blown upon, the beans are sufficiently parboiled. Add onion, diced salt pork, sugar, catsup, mustard, salt, and Worcestershire sauce. Place in greased casserole dish and decorate top with the salt pork strips. Bake, covered, at 275°F. 5 to 7 hours; uncover for last hour of cooking. Add additional water or stock if the beans become dry.

About 6 servings

NOTE: Mrs. Kennedy's original recipe is for double the amount given here. For 12 to 16 servings, double ingredients and bake 6 to 8 hours.

GREEN BEANS ANTIPASTO

1 package (9 ounces) frozen Italian-style green beans
2 tablespoons olive oil
1 tablespoon butter
2 small onions, sliced
½ green pepper, sliced
1 medium tomato
1 tablespoon sugar
1 tablespoon lemon juice
Salt to taste

Saute onion and green pepper in olive oil and butter about 5 minutes or until onion is transparent but not brown. Add 1 tomato that has been peeled and cut in chunks. Add sugar, lemon juice, and salt to taste. Add frozen green beans, separating them with a fork. Cover and simmer 15 to 20 minutes.

3 or 4 servings

Including Jacqueline Kennedy, almost everyone's favorite way of dressing green beans is to serve them Amandine. Here are two other recipes that lift green or string beans above the commonplace. The licorice flavoring of this one is very subtle and delicate.

LICORICE FLAVORED GREEN BEANS

Anise seed
1 cup dairy sour cream
2 tablespoons butter
1 teaspoon flour
¼ cup heavy cream
1 can (16 ounces) blue lake green beans, heated and drained
1 teaspoon chopped parsley

Pound anise seed into powder and add ½ teaspoon water. Add anise mixture to the sour cream some time before you are planning to use it and set aside at room temperature. Melt the butter in a saucepan. Stir in the flour and heat until bubbly. Blend in the heavy cream and bring to boiling. Remove from heat and stir in sour cream, a spoonful at a time. Serve sauce over hot beans and sprinkle with parsley.

4 servings

Lady Bird Johnson's
LIMA BEAN AND MUSHROOM CASSEROLE

1 package (10 oz.) frozen baby lima beans
¼ cup butter
5 oz. mushrooms, sliced
2 tablespoons flour
1 cup milk
¼ cup finely shredded cheddar cheese
¼ teaspoon salt
⅛ teaspoon black pepper
¼ teaspoon chili powder

Cook lima beans according to package directions and drain well. While lima beans are cooking, saute mushrooms in hot butter in a saucepan about 5 minutes. Blend in the flour. Heat until bubbly. Add milk gradually, stirring constantly. Bring to boiling and cook 1 to 2 min. Remove from heat and stir in the cheese and seasonings. Combine sauce and hot beans.

3 or 4 servings

In each of the following beet recipes, freshly cooked beets can be used interchangeably with the ones in the recipes, providing you reserve the beet juice, if necessary.

BEETS IN SOUR CREAM

- 1 jar or can (16 ounces) sliced red beets
- 4 tablespoons tarragon vinegar
- 3 tablespoons butter
- 3 tablespoons flour
- 1 cup dairy sour cream
- Caraway seed

Drain beet juice from beets, about 1 cup, and combine with the tarragon vinegar. Melt butter; stir in flour and heat until bubbly. Add beet juice gradually, stirring constantly. Bring to boiling continuing to stir; cook 1 to 2 minutes. Heat beets in this sauce. Garnish servings with heaps of sour cream and sprinkle caraway seed over all.

4 servings

BEETS IN ORANGE SAUCE

- 1 tablespoon cornstarch
- ¼ cup sugar
- ¼ teaspoon salt
- Pinch of ground ginger
- 2 tablespoons grated orange peel
- ¾ cup orange juice
- 3 tablespoons lemon juice
- ¼ cup melted butter
- 1 jar or can (16 ounces) beets, drained

Mix dry ingredients in a small saucepan; stir in grated peel, juices, and butter. Bring to boiling and cook, stirring constantly, until the sauce is thick and clear. Add beets, either small whole beets or cut in pieces if not baby beets. Heat beets in sauce. This is a quick and easy, yet colorful, sauce.

4 to 6 servings

BEETS IN RED WINE SAUCE

- 1 jar or can (16 ounces) beets, drained and ⅓ cup liquid reserved
- 2 tablespoons butter
- 1 shallot, minced
- 2 tablespoons flour
- ⅓ cup beef bouillon
- ⅓ cup red wine
- Light pinch of ground cloves (optional)

Melt butter in a saucepan and add minced shallot. Add flour, stirring constantly for 1 minute. Then add the liquids: reserved beet liquid, bouillon, and red wine. Bring to boiling stirring until sauce is smooth and thick. Add cloves, if desired. Add beets and heat thoroughly.

4 to 6 servings

One of the easiest, yet most attractive ways to serve vegetables is broccoli on artichoke bottoms. This can be prepared in the morning and served at night. You can obtain your rounds or bottoms from preparing globe artichokes; but it is easier to buy the cans of artichoke bottoms.

BROCCOLI BOUQUETS ON ARTICHOKE BOTTOMS

- 1 can artichoke bottoms
- 1 package (10 ounces) frozen chopped broccoli
- ½ cup Mornay Sauce (see recipe)

Cook chopped broccoli according to package directions and drain well. Take a small size ice cream scoop (or allow 1 heaping tablespoon) and pack broccoli tightly in it, then mound on a canned artichoke bottom which is about 2 inches in diameter. Spoon over the top of each broccoli-artichoke mound a small amount of Sauce. Then place the mounds on a baking sheet under the broiler and heat until sauce starts to bubble and browns a little. Remove from oven; store in refrigerator until ready to use. Then heat in a 350°F. oven and serve. *About 6 servings*

Mornay Sauce

- ¼ cup cold white sauce
- 2 tablespoons Hollandaise sauce
- 1 tablespoon grated Parmesan cheese

Mix all ingredients.

Mrs. L. B. Johnson's

SPINACH PARMESAN

- 3 pounds spinach
- 6 tablespoons shredded Parmesan cheese
- 6 tablespoons minced onion
- 6 tablespoons heavy cream
- 5 tablespoons melted butter
- ½ cup cracker crumbs

Cook the cleaned spinach until tender and drain well. Chop coarsely and mix in the cheese, onion, cream, and 4 tablespoons of the butter. Turn into a shallow 1-quart baking dish. Sprinkle with a mixture of the crumbs and remaining butter. Heat in a 375°F. oven 10 to 15 minutes.

8 servings

James Garfield was born Nov. 19, 1831, at Orange, Ohio, the last of the presidents to be born in a log cabin. His father died when he was two, and his mother guided him and his brothers and sisters through hardship, poverty, and uncertainty to a life of honored independence and strength.

20TH PRESIDENT

1881

While still in the Army, Garfield was elected to Congress. He resigned his commission and served in the House of Representatives for the next 18 years. He did notable service as chairman of the important Committee on Military Affairs.

Lady Bird Johnson's
DILLED OKRA

Fresh okra
1 teaspoon dill seed
1 hot red pepper
1 hot green pepper
2 cloves garlic
1 quart white vinegar
1 cup water
½ teaspoon salt, not iodized

Place ½ teaspoon of the dill seed in bottom of a large sterilized jar. Pack washed fresh okra as tightly as possible, being careful not to bruise the okra. Add remaining ½ teaspoon dill seed, peppers, and garlic. Bring to boiling vinegar, water, and salt and cover okra with mixture. Seal jar and allow to stand 2 weeks. Serve icy cold.

There are a great many recipes today that call for walnuts and pecans; try the unique flavor of filberts in these

FILBERT STUFFED BAKED ONIONS

6 large onions
½ cup chopped filberts
¼ cup melted butter
¼ cup herb-seasoned stuffing mix, crushed
Salt and pepper to taste
Dash of Beau Monde seasoning
2 tablespoons ground filberts
Light cream

Parboil onions in boiling, salted water for 5 minutes. While onions are cooking, lightly toast ½ cup chopped filberts. Drain onions and remove outer skin. Then scoop out the inside layer of the onions, leaving at least 3 large outer layers so onions will hold a firm shape. Mince a handful from the onion pulp. Add butter, chopped filberts, and crushed stuffing mix. Season with salt, pepper, and a dash of Beau Monde seasoning; mix. Fill the hollowed-out onions with the mixture and place them in a baking dish or casserole. Sprinkle the ground filberts on the onion tops. Pour about ½ inch of cream in the bottom of the casserole or baking dish. Bake at 375°F. 1 hour, or until onions test done. Spoon a little onion milk over the tops before serving.
6 servings

EASY EGGPLANT PUFF

1 cup cooked eggplant pulp
½ cup coarsely chopped onion
2 tablespoons cooking oil
1 cup boiling water
1 chicken bouillon cube
5 slices bread
1 egg, lightly beaten
Salt and pepper to taste

Pare, cube, and cook eggplant to obtain pulp. Saute onion in cooking oil until transparent. Dissolve bouillon cube in boiling water. Trim crusts from bread and soak the bread in the chicken broth. Combine eggplant pulp, onion, broken bits of the soaked bread and egg in a 1-quart greased casserole. Bake at 350°F. 30 to 40 minutes.
4 servings

The original State Dining Room at the White House became inadequate for the growing number of large dinner parties. It was enlarged and redecorated while Theodore Roosevelt was president and renovated during the Truman administration.

Epicurean Eggplant is a combination of eggplant, tomatoes, cheese, and garlic. It truly justifies its name. But for those who do not care for, or cannot eat tomatoes and garlic, the preceding recipe for Easy Eggplant Puff is an equally wholesome and delightful dish.

EPICUREAN EGGPLANT

    1 large eggplant
    2 tablespoons peanut oil
    2 cloves garlic, minced
    1 cup chopped onion
    1 can (10½ ounces) condensed tomato soup,
       undiluted
    2 tablespoons Spanish-style tomato sauce
    ¼ teaspoon salt
    ¼ teaspoon sweet basil
    2 tablespoons peanut oil
    1 cup herb-seasoned stuffing mix
    1 package (4 ounces) shredded pizza cheese
       or mozzarella
    2 tablespoons minced parsley
       Salt and pepper to taste

Wash, dry, and slice eggplant crosswise into ½-inch slices. Saute garlic and onion in peanut oil until onion is transparent and soft. Add tomato soup, tomato sauce, salt, and basil and cook slowly for 10 minutes; then remove from heat. Fry the eggplant slices in peanut oil until browned, 3 to 4 minutes on each side. Crush herb-seasoned stuffing mix until fine and add to it the following: pizza cheese or mozzarella, minced parsley, and salt and pepper to taste. Butter a 1½-quart deep-sided casserole. Place a layer of eggplant slices in the bottom; spoon a layer of tomato sauce over that, then a layer of the crumbed stuffing mixture. Keep alternating the layers until ingredients are used. Top with a light coating of shredded pizza cheese. Bake at 350°F. 20 minutes, or until cheese is brown and bubbly. *4 to 6 servings*

SWEET AND SOUR RED CABBAGE

    1 head (2 pounds) red cabbage, shredded
    4 tablespoons brown sugar
    1 teaspoon salt
    ½ cup meat stock
    ¼ cup cider vinegar
    4 slices bacon, diced
    4 tablespoons butter
    2 medium cooking (sour) apples, pared and
       sliced
    1 cup red wine

Discard tough, outer leaves of cabbage and shred, as for cole slaw. Combine brown sugar, salt, meat stock, and vinegar as a marinade. Let cabbage stand in marinade 1 hour or longer. (This cabbage is limp when served so can be marinated as long as you wish.) Cook bacon until crisp; drain bacon pieces, and pour off all but 2 tablespoons of bacon fat. Melt butter into bacon fat. Add cabbage, marinade and all. Arrange apples on top of cabbage. Cover and cook slowly 1 hour. Add 1 cup of red wine. Re-cover and simmer 30 minutes. *6 servings*

Carrot casserole tastes a lot better than it might sound, and it has all three ingredients necessary to a successful dish—flavor, texture, and color.

CARROT CASSEROLE

    ⅔ cup regular long-grain white rice
    2 cups milk
    1 cup water
    4 eggs (1 cup)
    1 to 4 tablespoons sugar
    1¼ teaspoons salt
    ¼ cup chopped toasted almonds
    3 cups coarsely shredded carrots
       Butter pieces

Cook rice in milk and water in the top of a double boiler over boiling water 35 minutes, or until rice is tender. Beat eggs with sugar and salt. Mix in cooked rice, almonds, and shredded carrots. Turn into a buttered shallow 1½-quart baking dish. Dot with butter. Bake at 350°F. about 1 hour. Serve hot. *6 to 8 servings*

The growing of fresh vegetables in early America was largely the province of the wealthy southern planter who had both favorable climate and labor for it. Plantation owners used to race one another to see who could bring in the earliest peas. Washington, who was especially fond of them, and Jefferson both recorded in diaries how early their peas, among other vegetables, were available each year. For a delicate and different flavor, try early, young, tender peas flavored with cumin seed, one of our earliest known spices. The seed resembles caraway seed, but has a delicate, subtle flavor of its own.

CUMIN FLAVORED SPRING PEAS

½ teaspoon cumin seed
¼ cup water
2 pounds fresh peas
¼ cup butter
6 green onions
½ cup heavy cream

Soak cumin seed in ¼ cup water. Shell 2 pounds of tender, young peas. One pound of peas unhulled is approximately 1 cup of young peas hulled. Melt butter in a saucepan. Chop green onions and saute them in the butter until transparent but not browned. Add cumin seed and water to the onion; add the peas. Add a little more water, if necessary. Cover and cook slowly (since this is almost waterless cooking) until almost done, about 10 to 20 minutes. Add heavy cream and heat thoroughly, but do not let cream boil.

4 servings

HASH BROWN POTATOES, MEN'S STYLE

6 medium white potatoes
1 cup boiling water
2 beef bouillon cubes
¼ cup butter
⅓ cup chopped white onion
⅓ cup chopped green pepper
Salt to taste
Freshly cracked black pepper

Pare and cube potatoes; put them in a covered saucepan with a cup of boiling water in which 2 beef bouillon cubes have been dissolved. Cover and cook over medium heat until potatoes are soft but not mushy, about 15 minutes. Most of the liquid will have been absorbed by the potatoes; pour off any excess. Melt butter in a heavy, iron skillet. Saute chopped onion until transparent, but not browned. Parboil half of a green pepper for 1 minute, then chop ⅓ cup from it. Add to onion and cook 1 minute longer. Chop cooked potatoes and add to skillet mixture. Sprinkle with salt to taste and some freshly cracked black pepper. Press the mixture together with a spatula. Cook over medium to low heat about 15 minutes or until a golden crust is formed on the bottom. You can lift the edges gently with a spatula from time to time to check the bottom. Remove from heat and invert into a large pie pan all at once. To serve, cut into wedges.

6 servings

NOTE: If desired, add 2 tablespoons chopped pimiento to skillet with chopped potato.

Chester A. Arthur, the fifth of nine children of Malvina Stone Arthur and William Arthur, a Baptist minister, was born in this cabin at Fairfield, Vt., on Oct. 5, 1830.

21ST PRESIDENT

1881-1885

Arthur always liked sports—especially fishing. He also appreciated fashionable clothes. While in the White House, he had his suits tailored in New York.

These potatoes are just what their name implies. The recipe is easily doubled to serve a group of 12 to 16, depending on the generosity of the helpings.

POTLUCK POTATOES

4 medium-large potatoes, pared (about 1½ pounds)
¼ pound sharp cheddar cheese, shredded
½ medium onion, grated (about 2 tablespoons)
¾ teaspoon salt
⅛ teaspoon pepper
1 tablespoon butter
1½ cups milk

Cook potatoes in a small amount of boiling salted water 15 minutes; remove and cool. When cool enough to handle, finely shred potatoes (should be about 4 cups). Mix potatoes, cheese, onion, salt and pepper; turn into a greased 1½-quart casserole or 10 x 6½ x 1¾-inch baking dish. Dot with butter. Pour milk over all. Bake at 300°F. at least 2 hours until milk is absorbed and top is browned.   *6 servings*

Potatoes Suzette often accompanied steaks served at the White House. Here are "twice-baked" potatoes as they were served to the Kennedys.

The Kennedys'
POTATOES SUZETTE

3 large Idaho potatoes
2 tablespoons butter
1 tablespoon heavy cream
1 egg yolk, well beaten
    Grated Parmesan cheese

Bake potatoes at 425°F. until done, about 1 hour. Cut in half lengthwise, scoop out inside and mash with butter, cream, and egg yolk. Beat mixture well and repack in potato shells. Top with a little grated Parmesan cheese. Return to the oven and heat until tops are golden brown.

6 servings

Teddy Roosevelt was so fond of sweet potatoes that they were sometimes referred to as "Roosevelt potatoes." During his tenure in the White House, sweet potatoes were shipped to him from the storage bins of his home, Sagamore Hill. (Asparagus and other vegetables were also shipped to the White House.) Had we been cook to the Roosevelts, we would have added egg to the following recipe and made the dish more of a pudding. But it is simple and has an interesting flavor, different than most sweet potato dishes. Help was plentiful in Teddy's day . . . we doubt that many people still want to take the time to grate raw sweet potatoes. It is rather hard work, but unfortunately it can't be done in an electric blender, as it changes the original consistency and flavor.

Teddy Roosevelt's
FAVORITE BAKED SWEET POTATOES

Mix to consistency of a good paste, and bake at 350°F. in a shallow baking dish a mixture of 6 medium **sweet potatoes,** scraped on a scraper, plus 2 spoonfuls of **water, salt, pepper,** and **sugar** to taste and a spoonful of **butter.**

4 to 6 servings

Somewhat more modern and definitely easier to prepare than Roosevelt potatoes, is the recipe that was used by the Hoovers. It was prepared by Mary Rattley, the Hoover family cook. Try it as a complement to poultry or wild game.

Herbert Hoover's
SWEET POTATOES

6 sweet potatoes
2 tablespoons butter
    Dash of nutmeg
    Salt to taste
½ cup cream
1 cup ground walnuts
    Marshmallows

Boil the sweet potatoes; peel and mash through a potato masher to remove all strings. Add the butter, nutmeg, salt, and cream enough to make a soft consistency. Blend in the ground walnuts. Put in a buttered baking dish and bake at 375°F. for 10 minutes, or just long enough for potatoes to heat thoroughly. Remove from oven and dot the top with marshmallows; return to oven and brown as for a meringue.   *6 to 8 servings*

Stephen Grover Cleveland, fifth child of a Presbyterian clergyman, was born in this three-story, white frame manse at Caldwell, N. J., on Mar. 18, 1837, and lived here until 1841, when his family moved to Fayetteville, N.Y., where the boy began to attend school.

22ND AND 24TH

PRESIDENT

1885-1889, 1893-1897

The first White House wedding took place in 1886 when, at the age of 49, Cleveland married 22-year-old Frances Folsom, the daughter of his former Buffalo law partner.

Wild rice was on the menu when ex-President Truman had dinner with President Kennedy at the White House, November 1, 1961. It was the first time anyone had invited the ex-president to dinner there since Truman had left office. As elegant as the wild rice, was the rest of the menu, too — mousse de crab, grouse Americaine, green beans, and a pineapple dessert accompanied by petits fours. Wild rice makes a wonderful party dish. But, since it is expensive, we suggest a party casserole of wild plus natural brown rice. The combination makes the casserole not only less prohibitive in cost, but also gives the dish an interesting texture.

WILD RICE CASSEROLE

½ cup wild rice, soaked overnight
½ cup brown rice, soaked overnight
1 cup sliced fresh mushrooms
½ cup chopped white onion
½ cup shredded sharp cheddar cheese
6 tablespoons cooking oil
1 cup hot chicken broth
2 tablespoons sherry
   Salt and pepper
   Pimiento strips

Soak wild and brown rice in water overnight, then drain. Combine rice, mushrooms, chopped onion, and shredded cheese in a 1½-quart casserole or an 8 x 8 x 2-inch baking dish. Stir in cooking oil, then hot chicken broth and sherry. Sprinkle with salt and pepper; garnish with pimiento strips. Bake at 350°F. 1 hour.

6 to 8 servings

A recipe that serves about 4, and is just as easy to follow and as tasty fresh as when it was written in a cookbook . . . way back in 1814.

Dolly Madison's

FRYING HERBS

1½ pounds fresh spinach
½ cup chopped parsley
6 green onions
   Salt to taste
   Butter

Wash and drain spinach leaves and parsley. Chop the parsley and onions, and sprinkle them among the spinach. Set them all on to stew with some salt and a bit of butter the size of a walnut; shake the pan when it begins to grow warm, and keep it closely covered over low heat until done. Serve with slices of broiled calf's liver, small rashers of bacon, and fried eggs; the latter on the herbs, the other in a separate dish.

About 4 servings

Mount Vernon, the beautiful plantation home of George and Martha Washington in Virginia, is a National Shrine. Washington enlarged the original residence and added many outbuildings including the kitchen (left) that is connected to the house by an open semi-circular arcade and the column-shaded piazza where guests frequently assembled before dinner.

Lady Bird Johnson's
SPINACH SOUFFLE

¼ cup chopped onion
1 tablespoon butter
3 eggs, separated
Mrs. L. B. Johnson's White Sauce
  (see recipe)
1 cup drained cooked spinach, chopped
½ cup grated Parmesan cheese

Saute onion in a small amount of butter. Beat egg yolks until thick and lemon colored. Stir into hot white sauce along with spinach and cheese. Fold in egg whites beaten until stiff, not dry, peaks are formed; turn into greased 1½-quart casserole. Set in pan of hot water and bake at 350°F. about 50 minutes. Serve at once.

About 6 servings

Mrs. L. B. Johnson's
White Sauce

2 tablespoons butter
2 tablespoons flour
1 cup milk or light cream
½ teaspoon salt
⅛ teaspoon pepper

Melt butter; stir in flour and heat until bubbly. Gradually add milk or light cream, stirring constantly; cook 1 to 2 minutes. Season with salt and pepper.

About 1 cup sauce

BROILED ZUCCHINI

6 medium-small zucchini
1 cup water
1 tablespoon chopped parsley
Pinch each of oregano and garlic salt
Salt and pepper to taste
¼ cup Spanish-style tomato sauce
4 tablespoons grated Parmesan cheese

Wash zucchini; cut off each end, and halve lengthwise, but do not pare. In a skillet, boil 1 cup of water; add zucchini, cover, and simmer until zucchini is tender but the pulp is still fairly firm. Add parsley, oregano, garlic salt, and salt and pepper to the tomato sauce. Drain zucchini and arrange skin side down in a shallow baking dish. Spoon the tomato sauce mixture over pulp side to cover. Sprinkle Parmesan cheese on top and broil until brown.   *6 servings*

Pat Nixon's

BAKED STUFFED TOMATOES

4 large or 6 medium tomatoes
4 to 5 slices bacon, cut in small pieces
6 tablespoons olive oil
¾ cup chopped onion
¼ pound fresh mushrooms, chopped
1 tablespoon *each* snipped chives and parsley
1 egg, beaten
½ teaspoon salt
⅛ teaspoon pepper

Cut away stem ends of tomatoes. Scoop out ¾ of each tomato, leaving about a ¾-inch wall (if using a paring knife to cut away interior, be careful not to pierce skin). Partially fry the bacon in a large skillet. Add 4 tablespoons of the olive oil; heat and mix in onion, mushrooms, chives, and parsley. Saute for 10 minutes, stirring the mixture occasionally. Remove skillet from heat. Quickly mix in the beaten egg, salt, and pepper. Immediately fill tomatoes and put into oiled baking dish. Top with **bread crumbs** and drizzle with remaining oil. Bake at 400°F. about 40 minutes.   *4 to 6 servings*

A bouquetierre of vegetables is an especially attractive service for a buffet table; and a busy hostess can prepare it ahead of time. It is not necessary to choose only the vegetables we have listed. As long as you have variation in color and texture, choose any group of vegetables you prefer.

BOUQUETIERRE OF VEGETABLES

Canned blue lake green beans
Glazed, cooked carrots
Cooked cauliflorets
Cooked broccoli spears
Broiled tomato halves
Artichoke hearts

There are no quantities listed because these would depend upon the number of people to be served and the number and sizes of the tray or trays to be used. Prepare your vegetables in the morning. Take the whole blue lake green beans and marinate them in an oil and vinegar or Bleu cheese salad dressing. Cook and glaze carrots. Cook either fresh or frozen cauliflorets and broccoli; drain. Sprinkle the tomato halves with grated Parmesan cheese, then, with your kitchen scissors, finely snip some fresh parsley over the top. Broil until the cheese bubbles, then remove from oven. You are now ready to assemble your bouquetierre. Take your largest silver or aluminum tray. Starting at the lower left hand corner and moving diagonally to the top right, place a row of broiled tomatoes in a line. On the right or "under" side of the tomato line, arrange a line of marinated green beans, alternately with a few cauliflorets. Beneath them in the lower right hand corner of the tray, bunch the glazed carrots cut in 3-inch pieces.

Now for the top of the tomato line. Just above the tomato line, but still following the diagonal lower left hand corner to upper right hand corner line, arrange a line of cooked broccoli spears. In the upper left hand corner of the tray, bunch the artichoke hearts garnished with a strip of pimiento on each. This may be done in advance of serving. When ready to serve, put silver tray in the oven and warm through. Offer a choice of 2 sauces in sauce boats with vegetables.

During Washington's presidency a popular social function was the weekly Tuesday afternoon reception held at his home. The painting "Lady Washington's Reception" by Daniel Huntington portrays Martha Washington receiving her guests.

Salads

AN OLD COOKBOOK refers to "breakfast salad." Another suggests that salad is a ladies' dish "seldom enjoyed by men!" Times and tastes do change, however, and these White House salads will be more often served with luncheon, supper, dinner or evening buffet, than with morning coffee.

Presidents and other men are likely to be enthusiastic in their praise of a tasty, eye-pleasing salad, whether it enhances a hearty meal or is served as a meal in itself. After all, Thomas Jefferson had maintained a kitchen garden at Monticello, and he often praised vegetables, especially greens, as the source of his health and long life.

Vinaigrette is a wonderful way to serve cooked vegetables, and a way of utilizing leftover ones. A choice of cooked asparagus, broccoli, cauliflower, carrots, onions, green beans, or any combination of them, may be used. Sliced cucumbers, artichoke hearts, and the elegant hearts of palm also lend themselves to this treatment.

ASPARAGUS VINAIGRETTE

Salad greens
3 large chilled spears of cooked asparagus
   per serving
1 or 2 hard-cooked eggs
Pimiento strips
Vinaigrette Dressing (see recipe)

Place asparagus on a bed of salad greens. Sieve egg over the spears; garnish with pimiento strips.

Shake dressing well before spooning over the asparagus salad.

Vinaigrette Dressing

¼ cup minced green onion
2 tablespoons minced parsley
1½ teaspoons sugar
1½ teaspoons salt
   Freshly cracked black pepper
2 tablespoons minced chives
1 tablespoon pickle relish
2 teaspoons capers (optional)
⅓ cup cider vinegar
1 cup salad oil

Combine all ingredients in a jar; cover. Shake vigorously and chill. *About 1½ cups dressing*

70

In the summertime it's always good to have a salad that's a one dish, easy-to-make meal. With a little garlic bread and a glass of chilled dry white wine you have a gourmet meal. This special chef's seafood salad is excellent for a summer buffet table as well . . . . and best of all . . . . it should be prepared ahead of time to be well chilled!

CHEF'S SEAFOOD SALAD

4 medium red potatoes, cooked, peeled, and
    diced
3 tomatoes, peeled and coarsely chopped
1 cup chopped green onion (with tops)
1 green pepper, chopped
1 hard-cooked egg, sieved
¼ cup sliced, pitted ripe olives
¼ cup olive oil
1 tablespoon tarragon vinegar
½ teaspoon salt
    Juice of a lemon
1 package (6 ounces) frozen Alaska king crab
1 cup fresh or frozen cooked lobster or 7
    ounces canned lobster meat
    Sprinkle of lemon juice
1 tablespoon chopped parsley
1 tablespoon chopped chives

Combine vegetables, egg and olives. Vigorously shake oil, vinegar, salt, and lemon juice, then toss with the vegetable mixture. Put the salad in a large bowl and cover with the thawed crab meat and the cooked lobster meat. Sprinkle lemon juice over the seafood and garnish with parsley and chives. Cover and chill. Just before serving toss the salad again.   *6 to 8 servings*

It takes a little time to chop the ingredients for this cole slaw variation, but it's well worth the effort. In making the dressing, use your most inexpensive salad dressing, the tangier the better!

BUFFET COLE SLAW

1 large head cabbage
1 medium onion
1 bunch parsley
½ pint salad dressing
6 tablespoons cider vinegar
    Sugar to taste (several tablespoons)

Chop the cabbage, onion, and parsley very fine. Toss with a mixture of salad dressing, vinegar, and sugar to taste.   *About 10 servings*

Note: To serve a crowd, double or triple recipe as required.

The earliest American cookbooks, if they mentioned spinach at all, carefully noted to wash it in "5 or 6 waters." That was necessary to remove all the sand and grit. Even today's pre-washed, packaged spinach should be carefully picked over leaf by leaf.

FLORENTINE SALAD

½ pound raw spinach
⅓ cup olive oil
1 ounce white wine vinegar
1 tablespoon sugar
½ teaspoon seasoned salt
½ teaspoon salt
1 teaspoon soy sauce
1 teaspoon prepared mustard
1 teaspoon lemon juice
1 small Italian (red) onion

Wash spinach, removing the larger stems and the larger veins. Tear into bite-size pieces. Combine all other ingredients, except onion, for a dressing and toss with the spinach, carefully coating each leaf. Garnish with paper-thin rings of the red onion.   *4 servings*

If you live in a metropolitan area, it may be possible to purchase mild, European garlic which has a more delicate flavor than the garlic buds generally found in food stores today. That is the basis of this wonderfully unusual green salad. If the mild European garlic is not available, you can approximate the same flavor with dry, imported, Belgian shallots, a bulbous member of the onion family that is faintly garlic scented. However, this salad, unlike most green salads, is one that does not lend itself to the substitution of ingredients.

OLD WORLD GARLIC SALAD

¼ cup finely chopped Belgian shallots or
    mild, European garlic
3 tablespoons pure olive oil
1 tablespoon white wine vinegar
2 teaspoons lemon juice
¼ teaspoon salt
1 large head romaine lettuce

Remove outer skin from the garlic cloves or shallots; then chop very finely. Combine olive oil, white wine vinegar, lemon juice, and salt into a dressing and marinate the shallots or garlic in it for 30 minutes. Tear lettuce into pieces. Toss gently with garlic and dressing mixture to coat evenly.   *4 servings*

One of the currently popular mixed green salads is the Caesar Salad, reputedly named after the West Coast chef who created it. It has many variations of which this is but one. It is generally prepared at table . . . . and with a great flourish!

CAESAR SALAD

   1 clove garlic
   ¼ cup salad oil
     Dash garlic salt
   3 slices bread, crusts removed
   2 cloves garlic, bruised
   ½ cup salad oil
   ¼ teaspoon salt
     Few grains pepper
   1 tablespoon Worcestershire sauce
   3 heads romaine lettuce, rinsed, dried, and
     chilled
   ¼ cup shredded Parmesan cheese
   6 anchovy fillets, chopped
   1 egg, coddled for 1 minute
   ¼ cup lemon juice

Make garlic croutons as follows: press or mash 1 clove garlic to a paste. Add to ¼ cup salad oil heated with the garlic salt. Fry bread cubes in the hot garlic oil until browned on all sides. Drain on absorbent paper. Add bruised cloves garlic to ½ cup salad oil; refrigerate several hours. Remove garlic; add salt, pepper, and Worcestershire sauce to the oil. Put crisp salad greens into a salad bowl. Add the cheese and anchovies; pour the flavored oil over all and toss. Break the coddled egg onto the greens; pour lemon juice directly over the egg. Toss again. Add reheated garlic croutons and toss again.

6 servings

Jacqueline Kennedy's
SALAD MIMOSA

A salad of **mixed greens** (varied) with an **oil and vinegar dressing**; topped by a generous sprinkling of **sieved hard-cooked egg yolks**. It's a simple but colorful salad and President Kennedy was partial to good green salads. Mimosa, which in French culinary means sprinkled with chopped hard-cooked egg yolk, has been used as a garnish on state-occasion dinners, also. The "starter" for the state dinner the Kennedys gave for Pakistan's President Ayub Khan, in 1961, was an avocado and crab meat mimosa . . . another interesting salad combination.

President Nixon and the First Lady stand on the South Portico of the White House with their daughters Tricia and Julie and their sons-in-law Edward Finch Cox and David Eisenhower.

President James Monroe did not create the following salad. In his day, all salads were cooked. Today's favorite tossed salads had yet to be developed. But we call this the President Monroe Salad because anchovies became a very popular and quite fashionable food during Monroe's administration.

President Monroe's

SALAD

1 large head romaine lettuce
1 flat can (2 ounces) anchovies, drained and chopped
1 cup sliced celery
2 medium tomatoes, coarsely chopped
1 small cucumber with peel, scored and sliced very thin
1 can (4 ounces) sliced ripe olives
Special Dressing (see recipe)

Tear lettuce into bite-size pieces and put into a salad bowl. Add anchovies to lettuce along with celery, tomatoes, cucumber, and olives. Toss with the Special Dressing after removing the mashed garlic.   *About 8 servings*

Special Dressing

Red wine vinegar
Olive oil
Salt to taste
1 clove garlic, mashed

Combine 3 parts vinegar, 1 part oil, salt to taste, and garlic in a screw-top jar. Cover jar tightly and shake well. Store covered in refrigerator. Shake dressing well before using.

This is a refreshing, sweet, tomato salad that MUST be prepared early. You find yourself with yet another recipe done that you don't have to worry about at the last minute.

TOMATO SALAD IN CASSEROLE

5 or 6 juicy, ripe tomatoes, sliced
½ cup chopped green pepper
½ cup chopped sweet Spanish onion
1 cup chopped celery hearts
Confectioners' sugar
Salt
1 tablespoon cider vinegar
3 tablespoons salad oil

Spread the bottom of a 1-quart earthenware casserole with a layer of the tomato slices. Mix the chopped pepper, onion, and celery and sprinkle a layer of the mixture over the tomatoes. Sprinkle sugar and salt over all. Start again with a tomato layer, a layer of chopped vegetables, and lightly sprinkle with sugar and salt; repeat in this order until the dish is full, ending with a tomato layer. Cover and place in the refrigerator until night, or at least 6 hours before serving. This will give the vegetables time to draw their own juices. Just before serving, mix 1 tablespoon cider vinegar with 3 tablespoons of salad oil. Pour over tomato casserole and whisk to the table. Serve the salad, over which you drizzle a little extra of the natural juices from the bottom of the bowl.   *8 servings*

Since 90 percent of our globe artichokes now come from California or the Southwest, it seems strange that they were a known favorite among our early Virginian presidents. Most of the statesmen had greenhouses in which they grew artichokes. Their early cookbooks contained rich recipes for artichoke pie, and even a recipe for dehydrating and preserving the vegetable. George Washington was known to prefer cooked artichoke rounds as his favorite salad. He would not have considered, though, eating them on uncooked lettuce, as we toss salads today. Because artichoke hearts are the feature of this delicious salad, we call it our

George Washington

SALAD

2 quarts mixed salad greens
2 cans (4½ ounces each) artichoke hearts
1 can (7¾ ounces) cut green asparagus
1 tablespoon seasoned salt
¼ teaspoon garlic salt
¼ teaspoon celery salt
¼ teaspoon garlic powder
¼ teaspoon paprika
¼ teaspoon sugar
¼ cup red wine vinegar
¾ cup salad oil

Wash, pat dry, and crisp your favorite combination of salad greens; tear into bite-size pieces. Drain artichoke hearts and coarsely chop them. Drain cut green asparagus spears. Add artichoke hearts and asparagus to salad bowl. Combine remaining ingredients as a dressing. Shake well, then toss some of the dressing with salad mixture until the greens are coated.   *About 6 servings*

Abraham Lincoln signed the proclamation which officially made Thanksgiving a national holiday. Some former presidents had observed Thanksgiving, but had done nothing officially about it. Ironically, in the early days of our country there were lots of people who were "con" Thanksgiving. Way back in John Quincy Adams' time (1826), a group of "pro" Thanksgiving people called upon President Adams to try to influence him to declare a Thanksgiving Day. He listened politely to the group's persuasions. But he came to an ultimate negative conclusion, stating that he was afraid the idea was too "regional" (New England). He called the idea of a Thanksgiving Day, a "novelty."

The traditional Thanksgiving Day foods — turkey, sweet potatoes, cranberries, succotash, and, of course, pumpkin pie are all indigenous to America. The following is a good cranberry salad for Thanksgiving. The cranberries are molded raw, giving this easy-to-prepare salad a wonderful flavor.

THANKSGIVING SALAD

- 1 package (6 ounces) lemon-flavored gelatin
- 2 cups boiling water
- 4 cups ground raw cranberries
- 2 oranges, coarsely ground
- 2 cups sugar
- 1 teaspoon salt
- 2 cups finely diced celery
- Whipped cream
- Mayonnaise

Dissolve gelatin in boiling water. Set in refrigerator until slightly thickened. Meanwhile, wash cranberries; put them through the medium blade of a food chopper. Quarter the oranges with skin; remove the white connecting membrane. Put the oranges through the coarse blade of the food chopper. Combine cranberries and oranges with sugar and salt; set aside while dicing the celery. Toss celery with the cranberry mixture. When the gelatin is slightly thickened, blend in cranberry-orange-celery mixture. Turn into a lightly oiled (with salad or cooking oil) glass dish 13 x 9 x 2-inches. Chill until firm. Cut into serving-size pieces. A good topping for this salad is a mixture of equal parts of whipped cream and mayonnaise.

12 servings

TOMATO ASPIC

- 3½ cups tomato juice
- ½ small onion, sliced
- 2 tablespoons lemon juice
- 1 small bay leaf
- ½ teaspoon salt
- ¼ teaspoon celery salt
- 5 drops Tabasco
- ¾ cup cold tomato juice
- 2 envelopes unflavored gelatin
- ½ cup sliced pimiento-stuffed olives
- ½ cup slivered blanched almonds
- Artichoke hearts, drained and cut in wedges

Combine the 3½ cups tomato juice with the next 6 ingredients in a saucepan; bring slowly to boiling over low heat. Meanwhile, soften gelatin in cold tomato juice in a bowl. Strain the hot tomato juice mixture into the softened gelatin, stirring until gelatin is completely dissolved. Cool and refrigerate until thoroughly chilled and slightly thickened. Meanwhile, distribute olives, almonds, and artichokes evenly over bottom of an 8 x 8 x 2-inch pan. Gently pour the cooled tomato mixture over all. Chill until firm. Cut into individual servings and place on bed of **salad greens.** Serve with mayonnaise, if desired.

About 8 servings

23RD PRESIDENT 1889-1893

Benjamin Harrison was born at North Bend, Ohio, on Aug. 20, 1833, on the estate of his grandfather William Henry Harrison, who was later President. Tutors and country-school teachers prepared him for Farmers College; later at Miami University in Oxford, Ohio, Harrison was graduated, in 1852, with a law degree.

As U.S. senator from Indiana, 1881-1887, Harrison supported labor legislation and successfully promoted legislation granting civil government to Alaska.

Cerise and gold silk, an Aubusson carpet, and 19th century furniture have re-created the Red Room of the White House as an Empire parlor typical of the era of President Monroe's administration.

Aspics and jellied salads were with us long before the use of sparkling gelatins as we know them today. Early Americans rendered their own gelatin from calves' feet. Andrew Jackson, while president, gave many large supper parties where the great horseshoe-shaped table was loaded with "every good and glittering thing French skill could devise, and at either end was a monstrous salmon in waves of meat jelly." The varieties of fruits, vegetables, seafoods, et cetera that blend agreeably in aspics are limitless and defy organization. Included are 3 well-flavored aspics with suggested garnishes.

BASIC ASPIC

1 beef bouillon cube
1 cup boiling water
1 tablespoon each cut-up onion, carrot, and celery
1 large sprig parsley
Pinch ground thyme
1 whole clove
5 whole peppercorns
1 small bay leaf
2 tablespoons unflavored gelatin
3 cups well-flavored chicken stock (fat removed), heated
1½ tablespoons lemon juice
⅛ teaspoon white pepper
¼ to ½ teaspoon salt
Whites of 2 small eggs, slightly beaten

Dissolve bouillon cube in boiling water; add onion, carrot, celery, parsley, and the next 4 ingredients. Simmer, covered, in a small saucepan 20 minutes. Strain and cool the broth. (Add water to make 1 cup.) Soften gelatin in cooled broth; dissolve completely in hot chicken stock. Add lemon juice, pepper, and salt to taste. Cool. Place in a heavy saucepan; add beaten egg whites slowly to broth over low heat stirring constantly with a wire whisk. Bring to a full rolling boil. Reduce heat and cook gently about 15 minutes. Remove from heat and set aside 30 minutes. Strain through a fine wire strainer lined with 3 or 4 thicknesses of cheesecloth. (For a sparkling transparent aspic, strain the broth through a funnel lined with 2 thicknesses of filter paper.) Chill until partially thickened. Pour aspic over chunks of **pink salmon** garnished with **sliced pimiento-stuffed olives** and **finely chopped chives** arranged in the bottom of an 8 x 8 x 2-inch pan. Or fold 1½ cups of assorted **finely shredded vegetables** (cabbage, carrots, celery, cucumber, and green pepper) into aspic and turn into a 1-quart ring mold or shallow pan. Chill until firm.

About 6 servings

NOTE: If aspic is to be used for molding salmon, 2 tablespoons dry white wine may be added to aspic after straining.

WHITE WINE ASPIC

1½ tablespoons unflavored gelatin
2 tablespoons sugar
¼ teaspoon salt
⅔ cup cold water
1¼ cups apple juice
1 cup Chablis or other dry white wine
1 tablespoon sweet pickle syrup
1 tablespoon lemon juice
½ cup dairy sour cream

Blend gelatin, sugar, and salt in a saucepan; add water. Place over low heat, stirring constantly, until gelatin and sugar are thoroughly dissolved. Stir in the next 4 ingredients. Chill until slightly thickened. Immediately blend with the sour cream. Pour into a fancy 1-quart ring mold and chill until firm. Unmold onto a serving plate and surround with **fresh fruits** such as peach or pear halves or wedges, bunches of Tokay or green grapes, sweet red cherries, orange segments, or other colorful fruits in season.

Or, if desired, fold 1½ cups shredded vegetables such as carrots, cabbage, cucumber, and green pepper into sour cream-gelatin mixture and turn into an 8 x 8 x 2-inch pan. Chill until firm, cut into squares, and serve in crisp lettuce cups.

About 6 servings

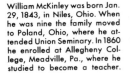

William McKinley was born Jan. 29, 1843, in Niles, Ohio. When he was nine the family moved to Poland, Ohio, where he attended Union Seminary. In 1860 he enrolled at Allegheny College, Meadville, Pa., where he studied to become a teacher.

W McKinley

25TH PRESIDENT

1897-1901

Elected a congressman from Ohio in 1876, McKinley soon gained prominence as an outspoken advocate of high-tariff legislation, which was finally passed by Congress in 1890.

Here's a Guacamole dressing that can be prepared ahead of time . . . a real boon for a busy hostess.

GUACAMOLE SALAD DRESSING

- 3 tablespoons finely minced
    green onion
- 2 tablespoons finely minced
    green pepper
- 1 large ripe avocado or 2 medium ones
- 1 tablespoon lime juice
- ¼ teaspoon salt
- ¼ teaspoon chili powder
    Dash of Tabasco
    Dash of pepper
    Clove of garlic, bruised
    Mayonnaise

Peel and mash a dead-ripe avocado. Add to onion and green pepper along with lime juice, salt, chili powder, Tabasco, and pepper. Mix well. Rub the inside of a small bowl with the garlic, then discard garlic. Put mixture into the bowl and cover with mayonnaise to prevent air from reaching avocado mixture. Chill thoroughly until serving time. Just before serving, stir mayonnaise into mixture. This recipe makes enough dressing to generously coat a quart of salad greens torn into pieces. Tomato wedges may be used as a garnish. *About 1 cup dressing*

HONEY CREAM DRESSING FOR FRUIT SALAD

- 1 cup mayonnaise
- 1 cup whipped cream
- ½ teaspoon salt
- 1 tablespoon lemon juice
- 2 tablespoons strained honey
- ¼ teaspoon ground nutmeg

Combine all ingredients and chill thoroughly before serving. *2 cups dressing*

Here is one of Dwight Eisenhower's favorites.

GREEN GODDESS SALAD DRESSING

- 4 anchovy fillets, finely cut or 2 tablespoons
    anchovy paste
- 3 tablespoons finely chopped green onion,
    including some tops
- 1 teaspoon chopped parsley
- 1 teaspoon lemon juice
- 1 tablespoon tarragon vinegar
    Dash of salt
    Dash freshly cracked pepper
- 1½ cups mayonnaise

Mix ingredients gently until blended; chill. This dressing goes especially well with a mixture of romaine, escarole, and chicory to make a green goddess salad. *About 1¾ cups dressing*

JULIENNE SALAD BOWL DRESSING

6 tablespoons cider vinegar
½ cup salad oil
1 tablespoon Worcestershire sauce
½ cup mayonnaise
1 tablespoon finely chopped chives
2 hard-cooked eggs, finely chopped

Combine all ingredients and chill before serving. Julienne salad bowl should include mixed greens with ham and chicken cut in thin strips (julienne). Accompany with the dressing.

1¾ cups dressing

Lyndon B. Johnson's
FAVORITE POPPY SEED DRESSING

1 teaspoon dry mustard
1 clove garlic
1 cup salad oil
¼ cup sugar
⅓ cup white vinegar
1 teaspoon grated onion or juice
1 teaspoon poppy seed
Pinch of salt

Put all ingredients in a jar; cover and shake well. Chill in refrigerator. Remove garlic. Shake well and serve with your favorite salad.

About 1½ cups dressing

ROQUEFORT DRESSING I

3 ounces Roquefort or blue cheese
1 cup salad oil
¼ cup sugar
¼ cup lemon juice
¼ cup catsup
1 teaspoon onion juice
1 teaspoon Worcestershire sauce

Blend all ingredients in an electric blender. Chill before serving.

About 2 cups dressing

ROQUEFORT DRESSING II

3 ounces Roquefort or blue cheese
¼ cup hot water
½ teaspoon salt
½ teaspoon garlic powder
Dash freshly ground black pepper
¼ cup sherry
1 cup salad dressing
¼ cup heavy cream

Blend all ingredients in an electric blender. Chill before serving. *About 2 cups dressing*

SOUR CREAM DRESSING, VERTE

1 cup dairy sour cream
2 tablespoons mayonnaise
1 tablespoon chopped parsley
1 tablespoon chopped chives
½ teaspoon salt
½ teaspoon sugar
½ teaspoon seasoned salt
Dash of Tabasco
Dash of garlic powder (optional)

Combine all ingredients and blend well. Will dress a quart of mixed salad greens.

1 cup dressing

YOGURT DRESSING

1 cup salad oil
¼ cup white wine vinegar
¼ teaspoon salt
Dash of white pepper
¼ teaspoon dry mustard
2 tablespoons sugar
2 tablespoons strained honey
1 cup yogurt

Combine salad oil, white wine vinegar, salt, pepper, dry mustard, and sugar. Blend in the honey, then the yogurt. Chill before serving.

2½ cups dressing

NOTE: Excellent with fruit or cheese salads.

At a formal dinner during Grant's administration, such as shown above, the State Dining Room and table were lavishly decorated.

The guests often were served a twenty-nine course dinner prepared under the direction of the White House chef, Melah.

Sauces

A GREAT CHEF IN A GREAT RESTAURANT has many advantages over the housewife (hostess) in her kitchen at home. The chef has access to many ingredients that are not commercially retailed; *glace de viande,* for example.

Few housewives have the time or the inclination to keep the necessary stock pot simmering.

A good, professional chef has years of experience as a *saucier* and does not necessarily follow level table measurements. Spices and herbs change in character and strength with age, and a chef varies these spices and herbs accordingly. It may be a "dash" of this, a "soupçon" of that, and a "trace" of both. The ingredient, and amount, that works one time may be insufficient or too much the next.

A good sauce takes preparation and, above all, good ingredients. Hannah Glass, in the 18th century cookbook, *The Art of Cookery Made Plain and Easy* discusses quite succinctly the art of the *saucier:* "You may leave out the wine, according to what use you want for it; so that really one might have a genteel establishment for the price the sauce of one dish comes to; but if gentlemen will have French cooks, they must pay for French tricks."

This cookbook includes the "French tricks" and, also, wherever possible, substitutes and alternates. There is, however, no substitute for fresh ingredients, especially herbs and spices.

We may largely thank, or blame, Thomas Jefferson for the French terms in our recipes and French names in our menus. Better still, we may thank or blame Julien, his chef. In 1779, when Jefferson returned to the fledgling United States after four years as Minister Plenipotentiary to France, he brought Julien with him. Julien remained as chef of the Jefferson households, including the eight years of Jefferson's presidency. Undoubtedly much French cuisine would soon have come to the United States under any circumstances, but let us give credit to Julien for bringing France to American kitchens nearly two centuries ago; including such delights as Rich Bechamel Sauce.

RICH BECHAMEL SAUCE

- 1 small onion, minced
- 3 tablespoons butter
- 2 tablespoons flour
- 1 teaspoon salt
- ¾ cup chicken stock
- 1 teaspoon lemon juice
- ¾ cup light cream
- 1 teaspoon brandy

Saute onion in butter until soft, but do not let onion brown. Blend in flour and salt. Gradually add chicken stock, stirring constantly; bring to boiling and cook 1 to 2 minutes. Remove from heat and strain through a fine sieve. Blend in the lemon juice. Add cream slowly, stirring constantly. Return to heat and cook slowly, stirring until sauce thickens. Blend in brandy.

1½ cups sauce

NOTE: To be used whenever a white sauce is needed.

A famous sauce of the broadest possible effectiveness, used successfully on almost everything: meats, poultry, game, vegetables, and in casseroles.

SOUBISE SAUCE

- 1 cup chopped onion
- 2 tablespoons butter
- 1 tablespoon water
- 1½ cups Rich Bechamel Sauce (omit brandy)

Saute chopped onion in the butter and water. Do not let onion brown. Stir in the Béchamel Sauce and simmer gently for 15 minutes or until onion is soft. Strain through a fine sieve before serving. Sauce may be pureed in a blender 1 minute and reheated. *1½ cups sauce*

POULETTE SAUCE

- 2 tablespoons butter
- ½ cup minced mushrooms
- 2 tablespoons flour
- 1 cup chicken or turkey stock
- 1 cup scalded milk
- 3 egg yolks, fork beaten
- 1 tablespoon strained lemon juice
- 2 teaspoons finely minced parsley

Melt butter in saucepan and saute mushrooms 3 minutes. Stir in flour. Gradually add blended chicken stock and milk, stirring constantly. Bring to boiling and cook 1 to 2 minutes. Blend a little sauce with the egg yolks, then return mixture to sauce, stirring constantly; cook about 5 minutes. Remove from heat and blend in the lemon juice. Garnish with the parsley.

2 cups sauce

NOTE: Poultry slices may be heated in the Poulette Sauce, sprinkled generously with Parmesan cheese, and set under the broiler until browned.

More than an excellent way to serve reheated leftover lamb, this savory East Indian sauce is good with poultry and eggs.

CURRY SAUCE

- 4 tablespoons butter
- ¼ cup finely minced onion
- ¼ cup finely chopped celery
- ½ teaspoon salt
  Dash of ground white pepper
  Dash of ground thyme
  Dash of ground mace
- 1 tablespoon curry powder
- 3 tablespoons flour
- 2 cups chicken stock
- 1 unpared, small, tart green apple, diced
- 2 teaspoons chopped chutney

Melt butter. Saute onion and celery in butter until just golden. Add salt, white pepper, thyme, mace, curry powder, and flour. Mix well to color. Slowly add the chicken stock, stirring constantly. Bring to boiling and cook 1 to 2 minutes. Add apple and chutney to sauce and heat gently 5 minutes, stirring constantly. *2 cups sauce*

The original source remains a mystery, but this recipe will be welcomed by those who would avoid the trouble—or sometimes the uncertainty—of preparing a classic Hollandaise. The flavor is quite comparable.

EASY HOLLANDAISE SAUCE

- ½ cup softened butter
- 3 tablespoons lemon juice
- 3 egg yolks

Place all ingredients in a small saucepan and allow to stand for at least 30 minutes. Five minutes before serving, cook over gentle heat, stirring constantly with a wooden spoon. In 2 or 3 minutes, Hollandaise sauce will thicken; serve at once. *About ⅔ cup sauce*

Theodore Roosevelt was born on Oct. 27, 1858, in the family home on East 20th Street in New York, the second of four children. He was reared there in an atmosphere of culture, dignity, and restraint.

Theodore Roosevelt

Roosevelt left the White House in 1909 only to be renominated in 1912 by the Progressive, or Bull Moose, party. But he failed to win the election.

Because you will use it so often in so many ways, it's important that this basic sauce may be stored up to a week refrigerated, or can be frozen for future use.

BASIC BROWN SAUCE

- ¼ cup chopped green onion (some tops)
- ½ cup chopped celery
- ½ cup chopped carrot
- 2 tablespoons cooking oil
- 2 quarts water
- 3 beef bouillon cubes
- 3 chicken bouillon cubes
- 1 small bay leaf
  Pinch of ground thyme
  Dash of freshly ground black pepper
  Dash of monosodium glutamate
- 2 tablespoons tomato sauce
- ½ cup water
- ¼ cup flour

Using a large saucepot, saute onion, celery, and carrot in cooking oil until dark brown, but not burned. Add water, beef and chicken bouillon cubes, bay leaf, thyme, black pepper, and monosodium glutamate. Bring to boiling and then simmer until stock is reduced by half. Strain. Stir in tomato sauce and bring to boiling. Shake vigorously in a screw-top jar the water and flour. Add gradually to boiling mixture, stirring constantly. Cook 1 to 2 minutes and simmer about 30 minutes, stirring occasionally.

1 quart sauce

As the name suggests, it is most famous as a sauce for wild game. Use it with eggs, too.

CHASSEUR (Hunter's) SAUCE

- ¼ cup butter
- 1 Belgian shallot, finely minced
- 1 cup sliced fresh mushrooms
- ½ teaspoon salt
  Dash of freshly ground pepper
- ½ cup dry white wine
- 1 cup Basic Brown Sauce
- 2 tablespoons tomato sauce
- 2 tablespoons butter
- 1 tablespoon finely chopped parsley

In ¼ cup butter, saute finely minced shallot and mushrooms, adding salt and pepper. When mushrooms are golden brown, stir in the wine and reduce by half. Blend in the brown and tomato sauces. Bring to boiling, then simmer gently for 15 minutes, stirring occasionally. Add butter and parsley. Cook 2 minutes longer, stirring until blended.

2 cups sauce

When serving grilled fish fillets, cooked seafood, crab, shrimp and lobster, great chefs have confidently rested their reputations on the perfection of this most appropriate sauce.

SAUCE CARDINAL

2 tablespoons butter
2 tablespoons flour
¼ teaspoon salt
  Dash of ground white pepper
½ cup hot fish stock
1 cup heavy cream
1 cup cooked lobster meat, cut in
  coarse dice
  Sliced, pitted ripe olives
  Red food coloring (optional)

Melt butter over low heat. Stir in flour, salt, white pepper to make a **roux**. Cook over low heat, adding fish stock and cream gradually, while stirring constantly. Bring to boiling and cook 1 to 2 minutes. Add cooked lobster meat and reheat without bringing to a boil. Garnish with sliced, pitted ripe olives. In France, the garnish is chopped truffles, but in America, truffles are very expensive. Chefs pound lobster coral, or roe, with lobster shell in a mortar to give Cardinal Sauce its pink color. A few drops of red food coloring will produce the same effect.   *1½ cups sauce*

A sophisticated embellishment for grilled meats, sauteed meats, grilled fish, it was highly regarded as a steak sauce when the Kennedys were in the White House.

BEARNAISE SAUCE

1 tablespoon chopped shallots
1 teaspoon dried tarragon (or 2 tablespoons
  chopped fresh)
2 bruised peppercorns
⅓ cup white wine vinegar
4 egg yolks
2 tablespoons water
1 cup butter
1 tablespoon minced parsley
  Dash lemon juice
  Salt to taste
  Dash ground white pepper

Combine finely chopped shallots, ½ the tarragon, bruised peppercorns, and white wine vinegar in a saucepan; cook until vinegar is reduced to 2 tablespoons. Cool slightly. Beat egg yolks in water and gradually add egg yolks to the vinegar, stirring constantly. Heat in a double

boiler, over simmering water, stirring constantly with a perforated spoon or wire whisk until mixture is creamy and thickened. Cool slightly; melt and skim butter, then add butter slowly to sauce, beating all the while. Strain the sauce; add parsley and remaining tarragon as garnish. Finish sauce with a dash of lemon juice, salt and pepper.   *About 2 cups sauce*

NOTE: Sauce may be covered and kept warm 15 to 30 minutes over hot water; stir occasionally.

Highly recommended with variety meats, such as kidneys and liver, it also spices leftover pork.

SAUCE PIQUANTE

¼ cup dry white wine
1 tablespoon vinegar
1 tablespoon butter
2 teaspoons minced shallot
1 cup Basic Brown Sauce (page 80)
1 tablespoon finely minced parsley
1 tablespoon tart pickle relish or
  2 tablespoons minced sour gherkins

Combine wine, vinegar, butter, and shallot. Boil until liquid is reduced by half. Stir in brown sauce, parsley, and pickle relish. Serve hot.
                         1 cup sauce

Here's how master chefs add a touch of magnificence to tender, flavorsome filet of beef or filet mignon.

MARCHAND DU VIN (Wine Dealer's) SAUCE

1 Belgian shallot, finely minced
4 tablespoons butter
1 cup dry red wine
1 cup Basic Brown Sauce (page 80)
1 tablespoon meat extract
1 tablespoon chilled butter
  Dash of lemon juice
1 teaspoon finely minced parsley

Saute the shallot lightly in butter. Add wine and boil down until volume is reduced by half. Stir in the brown sauce and meat extract, and simmer gently 10 minutes. At the last, stir in butter until melted, and sharpen with a dash of lemon juice. Blend in the parsley.
                         1½ cups sauce

Bordelaise Sauce

Follow recipe for Marchand Du Vin Sauce using **red Bordeaux wine.**

William Howard Taft was born at Cincinnati, Ohio, on Sept. 15, 1857. Graduated from Yale University in 1878, he went on to Cincinnati Law School for two years. He was admitted to the Ohio bar in 1880 and did some political speech-making for the Ohio Republican party's state committee.

27TH PRESIDENT

1909-1913

As President, Taft attempted to carry on Roosevelt's progressive program but aroused opposition by supporting tariff reform in the long-debated Payne-Aldrich bill.

Good on cold meats, shellfish, raw vegetable or chicken salad.

REMOULADE SAUCE

- 1 cup mayonnaise
- 4 small sweet pickles, minced
- 2 tablespoons lemon juice
- 1 tablespoon minced onion
- 1 tablespoon minced green pepper
- 1 tablespoon horseradish mustard
- 1 teaspoon anchovy paste
- 1 teaspoon minced fresh tarragon

Combine all ingredients and chill thoroughly.

About 1½ cups sauce

Created to meet a need . . . the one delectable sauce that baked fish needs!

VERONIQUE SAUCE .

- 4 tablespoons butter
- ¼ cup minced green onion
- 1 cup mushrooms, cut in ¼-inch dice
- 1 small clove garlic, minced
- 2 tablespoons flour
- 1 can (8¾ ounces) white seedless grapes
- 1 cup canned beef gravy
- 2 tablespoons sweet vermouth

Melt 2 tablespoons butter in a skillet and saute onion, mushrooms, and garlic until onion is soft.

In a separate saucepan, melt the other 2 tablespoons butter; add flour and stir to make a **roux** (thickening). Drain juice from the grapes (about ½ cup juice) and adding slowly, blend into the **roux**. Bring to boiling and cook 1 to 2 minutes. Stir thickened grape juice into onion mixture. Cook over low heat while slowly adding and blending in the beef gravy. Add grapes and heat thoroughly. Just before serving stir in the vermouth.

About 2½ cups sauce

A superb steak sauce, it has been adapted to the glorification of grilled pork.

SAUCE ROBERT

- 3 tablespoons butter
- ¼ cup finely chopped onion
- ½ cup dry white wine
- 2 tablespoons white wine vinegar
- 1 cup Basic Brown Sauce (page 80)
- 2 tablespoons tomato sauce
  Salt and pepper
- 1 tablespoon prepared mustard

Saute onion in butter until golden. Add wine and vinegar and reduce by half. Stir in the brown and tomato sauces. Add salt and pepper to taste. Simmer slowly for 10 minutes. At the last moment, blend in the mustard.

About 1½ cups sauce

Cakes

THERE ARE THREE LIKELY SOURCES of the magnificent cakes selected for this cookbook: (1) a succession of outstanding White House chefs whose pride and reputations rested solidly on the excellence of fancy cakes served at the end of the meal and, therefore, the course most likely to be remembered; (2) the First Ladies who brought to the White House with them their personal recipes for the Presidents' favorite cakes . . . Grace Coolidge's Vermont Cake being a fine example; (3) the famous American "sweet tooth" that has been shared by virtually every President since George Washington enjoyed Martha's Fruited White Cake.

You'll want to add these recipes to your repertoire of rich baked masterpieces.

George Washington returned to Mount Vernon at the close of his presidency in March of 1797. But guests and strangers were more numerous than ever. In writing to an acquaintance that summer he revealed that that particular evening was to be the first time in 20 years that he and Martha would be dining alone! Entertaining on such a large scale (30 people were an average for dinner), necessitated great quantities of cooking. Cake recipes have come down to us in Martha's own hand quoting 40 eggs, separated, 4 pounds of butter, et cetera. Of course, 40 eggs in Martha's day were more the size of pullet eggs today, but even so . . . Here is an authentic recipe of Martha's for a "Great Cake" which she also called her "rich, black cake."

Martha Washington's
RICH BLACK CAKE

Take 20 **eggs,** divide the whites from the yolks, and beat the whites to a froth. Then work 2 pounds **butter** to a cream, put the whites of eggs to it, a spoonful at a time, until well mixed. Then put 2 pounds of **sugar,** finely powdered, in it in the same manner. Then add the yolks of **eggs,** well beaten, 2½ pounds of **flour,** and 5 pounds of **fruit.** Add to this ¼ ounce of **mace,** a **nutmeg,** grated, ½ pint of **wine,** and some French **brandy.** Five and one-quarter hours will bake it.

A variation of this cake was served as dessert, for luncheon to Her Majesty, Queen Elizabeth and Prince Philip, the day they arrived at the White House and lunched with President and Mrs. Eisenhower. Martha Washington's fruit cakes, for that's what they are, are too unwieldy to bake in today's home oven. But reduced to portions that would be popular today, Martha's fruit cake modifies to this:

Martha Washington's
FRUITED WHITE CAKE

- 1 cup butter
- 1 cup sugar
- 5 eggs, separated
- 2½ cups sifted all-purpose flour
- 1 teaspoon ground mace
- ¼ teaspoon ground nutmeg
- 1 cup diced assorted candied fruits
- 2 tablespoons red wine
- 2 teaspoons brandy

Cream butter; add sugar gradually beating thoroughly. Add egg yolks, one at a time, beating until fluffy after each addition. Sift spices with the flour. Combine flour with fruits, then add all to the butter-egg mixture and mix well. Blend in the wine and brandy. Fold in egg whites, beaten until stiff, not dry, peaks are formed. Turn into a greased (bottom only) and lightly floured 9-inch tubed pan. Bake at 325°F. about 1¼ hours or until cake tester inserted in cake comes out clean. Place pan on a rack and cool cake completely in pan. Frost as desired.

One 9-inch tubed fruit cake

Grace Coolidge's Vermont Cake is a delightfully light angel food variation. It bakes as well today as it did many years ago. Separate your eggs while they are still cold; they separate easier. Then bring whites to room temperature before beating them. Do not skip the extra sifting of the sugar and flour.

Grace Coolidge's
VERMONT CAKE

 1 cup plus 3 tablespoons sifted cake flour
1½ cups sugar
1½ cups egg whites
 ¼ teaspoon salt
1¼ teaspoons cream of tartar
1¼ teaspoons vanilla extract
 ½ teaspoon almond extract

Sift the flour and ¾ cup sugar together 4 times. Beat egg whites slightly. Add the salt and cream of tartar. Beat until stiff, not dry, peaks are formed. Fold in the remaining ¾ cup sugar, about 3 tablespoons at a time. Fold in the extracts. Now fold in the flour-sugar mixture, sifting a little at a time over the batter and folding it in evenly. Turn batter into an ungreased 10-inch tubed pan. With a spatula, cut down through the batter all the way around to remove any air bubbles. Bake at 350°F. about 45 minutes. Remove from oven, invert on a cake rack or over a bottle, and cool for an hour; then loosen with spatula to remove cake. Ice with 1 pint of **whipped cream** flavored with a light grating of **lemon peel** and **almond extract** to taste. Decorate with 1 pound peeled **white grapes.** *One 10-inch tubed cake*

BOURBON TORTE

 6 egg yolks
 2 tablespoons bourbon whiskey
 1 teaspoon vanilla extract
 1 cup sugar
 1 cup finely ground nuts
 ¾ cup finely ground, dried rye bread crumbs
 6 egg whites
 ½ cup sugar

Beat egg yolks, bourbon, and vanilla extract; add the 1 cup sugar gradually beating until thick. Mix in nuts and crumbs. Beat egg whites until frothy; gradually add remaining ½ cup sugar beating constantly until stiff peaks are formed. Fold into egg yolk mixture. Grease (bottoms only), waxed-paper line, and grease again three 8-inch round layer-cake pans. Turn cake mixture into pans spreading evenly to edges, and bake at 350°F. about 30 minutes, or until cake tests done. Set on wire rack 15 minutes before removing from pans to cool completely. This cake is rich and should be iced with a very thin **chocolate icing.** Or spread **whipped cream** between layers. *One 8-inch 3-layer cake*

Woodrow Wilson was born on Dec. 28, 1856, at Staunton, Va., the son of a Presbyterian minister. His childhood was spent in Georgia and the Carolinas, and he was reared in an atmosphere of culture, refinement, and piety.

28TH PRESIDENT

1913-1921

Wilson, first U.S. president to travel to Europe, met with Clemenceau, Lloyd George, and Orlando at Paris and signed the peace treaty in Versailles' Hall of Mirrors, 1919.

PRAIRIE CAKE WITH BURNT SUGAR TOPPING

    1 cup quick cooking rolled oats
 1¼ cups boiling water
    ¼ pound (½ cup) butter or margarine,
        softened
    1 teaspoon vanilla extract
    1 cup granulated sugar
    1 cup packed brown sugar
    2 eggs
 1⅓ cups sifted all-purpose flour
    1 teaspoon baking soda
    1 teaspoon ground cinnamon
       Burnt Sugar Topping (see recipe)

Stir the oats into the boiling water and cook 1 minute; cover and let cool for 20 minutes. Meanwhile, cream butter and vanilla extract; gradually add granulated and brown sugars, creaming thoroughly. Beat in the eggs, one at a time. Blend in the oatmeal. Sift flour, baking soda, and cinnamon together. Add to butter-oatmeal mixture in halves and beat thoroughly to blend. Turn into a greased (bottom only) and lightly floured 11 x 7 x 1½-inch pan; bake at 350°F. about 45 minutes, or until cake tests done. Spread topping onto hot cake. Return to oven for 10 minutes, or put under broiler with top about 4 inches from heat source until topping starts to bubble.   *One 11 x 7-inch cake*

Burnt Sugar Topping

    3 tablespoons butter or margarine
    ⅔ cup packed brown sugar
    3 egg yolks
    1 cup shredded coconut
    1 cup finely chopped nuts

Blend butter with brown sugar. Add egg yolks and beat well. Blend in coconut and nuts.
                        About 2 cups topping

James Madison, called "The Father of the Constitution," married the widow, Dolly Payne Todd, in October, 1794, at a beautiful Virginia plantation named "Harewood," situated in then Jefferson County, Virginia, and now part of West Virginia. Harewood was the home of President Washington's nephew. It was both a beautiful and an historic setting for a wedding. The estate had once belonged to Washington's older brother, Samuel. Lafayette had visited there and had gifted the plantation with a mantel of carved crystalline stone. The then Congressman Madison

and his bride were married before the elaborate mantel. No doubt Harewood Plantation Pound Cake was served at the wedding feast, for it was the most popular cake of the day. This is the authentic recipe that has been handed down from Harewood Plantation.

PLANTATION POUND CAKE

    1 pound butter
    ½ teaspoon lemon extract
    ½ teaspoon freshly grated nutmeg
 10 eggs, separated
    1 pound confectioners' sugar, sifted
    1 pound all-purpose flour,
        sifted (4 cups)
    1 tablespoon French brandy

Cream the butter with the extract and nutmeg until butter is soft as thick cream. Beat egg yolks until thick. Mix alternately into the creamed butter the sugar, flour, and egg yolks and beat all together thoroughly. Mix in the brandy. Gently fold in the well-beaten egg whites until well blended. Grease and dust with flour a 10-inch tubed pan or two 9 x 5 x 3-inch loaf pans. Pour in the batter and bake at 300°F. about 1 hour and 45 minutes or until cake tests done.
                One 10-inch tubed cake or 2 loaves

This modernized version of pound cake produces a light-textured cake that is a perfect accompaniment to coffee or tea.

POUND CAKE

    2 cups sifted all-purpose flour
    ¾ teaspoon baking powder
    ¼ teaspoon salt
    ¼ teaspoon ground mace
    1 cup butter
    2 teaspoons grated lemon peel
 1½ teaspoons vanilla extract
    ½ teaspoon almond extract
    1 cup plus 2 tablespoons sugar
    4 eggs, well beaten

Sift the flour, baking powder, salt, and mace together. Cream butter, lemon peel, and extracts. Add sugar gradually beating until fluffy after each addition. Add beaten eggs in thirds, beating thoroughly after each addition. Add flour mixture in thirds beating until blended after each addition. Turn batter into a greased (bottom only) 9 x 5 x 3-inch loaf pan. Bake at 325°F. 1 hour and 10 minutes, or until cake tests done.
                        One 9 x 5-inch loaf cake

When the six high-spirited children of Teddy Roosevelt played in the stately White House, there was unprecedented light and life, joy and youthful gaiety, and family dining as truly American as maple syrup!

MAPLE-BUTTERNUT CAKE

2⅔ cups sifted cake flour
1 tablespoon baking powder
¾ teaspoon salt
¾ cup butter
⅔ cup packed light brown sugar
7 egg yolks, well beaten
⅔ cup milk
⅔ cup maple syrup
½ cup butternuts or walnuts, coarsely chopped
Maple Sugar Frosting (see recipe)
½ cup coarsely chopped butternuts or walnuts

Sift together flour, baking powder, and salt; set aside. Cream butter until softened. Add sugar gradually, beating constantly until fluffy. Add egg yolks in thirds, beating thoroughly after each addition. Blend milk and maple syrup. Beating only until smooth after each addition, alternately add dry ingredients in fourths and liquid in thirds to creamed mixture. Blend in ½ cup of the nuts. Turn into three greased (bottoms only), waxed-paper lined, and greased again 8-inch round layer-cake pans. Bake at 350°F. 45 to 50 minutes, or until cake tests done. Cool layers 10 minutes on wire racks before removing from pans. When layers are cooled, fill and frost with Maple Sugar Frosting. Sprinkle remaining nuts around outside edge of top.

One 8-inch 3-layer cake

Maple Sugar Frosting

1 cup sugar
1 cup packed maple sugar (see note)
1 cup dairy sour cream

Combine ingredients in a saucepan. Set over low heat and stir until sugar is dissolved. Increase heat and bring to boiling. Set a candy thermometer in place so that bulb does not touch bottom or sides of pan. Continue cooking without stirring to 238°F. (soft ball stage: a few drops of mixture form a soft ball in very cold water. Remove from heat while testing). During cooking, wash sugar crystals from sides of pan occasionally with pastry brush dipped into water. Change water after each washing. Remove saucepan to a wire rack and cool to lukewarm (about 110°F.) without stirring or moving the pan. Beat vigorously with wooden spoon or electric beater until mixture begins to lose its gloss and is of spreading consistency. Spread on cake immediately. If frosting becomes too thick to spread, beat in a few drops of **cream** or **milk.**

Enough to frost sides and tops of three 8-inch round cake layers

NOTE: If maple sugar is available only in solid form, grate, using a fine grater, before using. Or heat over simmering water until sugar is softened, then force through a fine sieve.

Not many recipes of McKinley's have come down to us, but here is one — the authentic recipe for his favorite cake. Other Presidents who loved this old-fashioned type of chocolate cake were Benjamin Harrison and Teddy Roosevelt. This recipe is one that great-grandmother might have favored, yet it has a moist, rich, up-to-date flavor.

President McKinley's

FAVORITE CHOCOLATE CAKE

6 squares (6 ounces) unsweetened chocolate
2 egg yolks
½ cup hot water
½ cup butter
1½ teaspoons vanilla extract
2 cups packed brown sugar
2 cups sifted cake flour
1 teaspoon baking soda
½ teaspoon salt
1 cup sour milk (see note)

Melt chocolate over hot water. Stir in egg yolks, then very slowly add the ½ cup hot water, stirring constantly. Cook and stir until smooth and thickened. Set aside to cool. Cream butter and vanilla extract; add sugar gradually, creaming thoroughly after each addition. Blend in cooled chocolate mixture. Sift flour, baking soda, and salt together. Add alternately with sour milk to butter-sugar mixture beginning and ending with dry ingredients and beating until blended after each addition. Turn into 2 greased (bottoms only) and greased waxed-paper lined 8-inch round layer-cake pans. Bake at 350°F. 25 to 30 minutes, or until cake tests done. Cool on wire rack 10 minutes before removing from pans.

Two 8-inch layers

NOTE: To sour milk, add sweet milk to 1 tablespoon cider vinegar, in a measuring cup, to 1-cup level; stir.

Warren Gamaliel Harding was born Nov. 2, 1865, near Caledonia, Ohio, the eldest of eight children. At 14, he enrolled at Ohio Central College at Iberia. Graduated in 1882, he then accompanied his family to Marion, where his father, a doctor, moved to practice medicine.

As Republican presidential candidate in 1920, Harding conducted a "front-porch" campaign from his home in Marion and emphasized "return to normalcy."

Mary Todd made this cake for Abraham Lincoln before their marriage and he declared it "the best in Kentucky!"

Abraham Lincoln's

FAVORITE CAKE

- 1 cup butter
- 1½ teaspoons vanilla extract
- ¼ teaspoon almond extract
- 2 cups sugar
- 3 cups sifted all-purpose flour
- 1 tablespoon baking powder
- ¼ teaspoon salt
- 1 cup milk
- 1¼ cups toasted blanched almonds, chopped fine
- 6 egg whites

Cream butter and extracts; add 1 cup sugar gradually creaming until light and fluffy after each addition. Sift flour, baking powder, and salt together. Add alternately in thirds with milk to creamed mixture. Mix in nuts. Beat egg whites until frothy; add 1 cup sugar gradually beating well after each addition. Continue beating until stiff peaks are formed; fold into batter. Turn into a greased (bottom only) and greased waxed-paper lined 10-inch tubed pan. Bake at 350°F. about 1 hour, or until cake tests done. Cool 15 minutes in pan before removing cake to wire rack. When cool, ice cake with a **boiled icing** to which add ½ cup **candied pineapple** and ½ cup **candied cherries,** chopped fine. *One 10-inch tubed cake*

Grover Cleveland

CAKE

- 3 cups sifted all-purpose flour
- 2 cups sugar
- 1 cup butter or margarine
- 2 tablespoons ground cinnamon
- 4 teaspoons cocoa
- 1 teaspoon ground nutmeg
- ⅛ teaspoon ground cloves
- 1 teaspoon baking soda
- ½ teaspoon baking powder
- ⅛ teaspoon salt
- 1 cup pecans, chopped
- 1 cup dark seedless raisins
- 2 cups buttermilk

Sift flour and sugar together into a large bowl. Cut in butter or margarine with pastry blender or two knives until pieces are the size of small peas. Measure 1 cup of the crumb mixture and set aside. To remaining mixture, add a blend of cinnamon and next six ingredients; mix well. Stir in nuts and raisins. Make a well in center of dry ingredients and add buttermilk all at one time. Stir until just blended. Turn batter into greased, waxed-paper lined, and greased again 13 x 9½ x 2-inch pan. Sprinkle top with the reserved crumb mixture. Bake at 350°F. 1 hour, or until cake tests done. Cool cake 10 minutes in pan on wire rack before removing from pan to cool completely. *One 13 x 9-inch cake*

A rather modernized variation of the McKinley cake is Mrs. Eisenhower's rich and moist devil's food recipe.

Mrs. Eisenhower's

DEVIL'S FOOD CAKE

2½ cups sifted cake flour
1¼ teaspoons baking powder
 1 teaspoon baking soda
 ¼ teaspoon salt
 ½ cup butter
 1 teaspoon vanilla extract
 2 cups sugar
 3 eggs, separated
 ⅔ cup cocoa dissolved in ½ cup boiling water
 1 cup sour milk (see note page 86)
   Mrs. Eisenhower's Seven-Minute Frosting
   (see recipe)

Sift flour, baking powder, baking soda, and salt together. Cream butter and vanilla extract. Add sugar gradually beating until blended after each addition. Beat in egg yolks, one at a time. Add cooled cocoa mixture; beat until well blended. Add flour mixture in thirds alternately with milk, beginning and ending with flour. Fold in egg whites beaten until stiff, not dry, peaks are formed. Turn batter into two greased (bottoms only) 9-inch layer-cake pans. Bake at 375°F. 25 to 30 minutes. Cool before filling and frosting with Seven-Minute Frosting.

One 9-inch 2-layer cake

Mrs. Eisenhower's

Seven-Minute Frosting

 2 egg whites, unbeaten
1½ cups sugar
 5 tablespoons cold water
 2 teaspoons light corn syrup or ½ teaspoon
   cream of tartar
   Few grains salt
 1 teaspoon vanilla extract

Combine all ingredients except vanilla extract in top of a double boiler. Stir until sugar is dissolved, then place over briskly boiling water. Beat with rotary or electric beater until stiff enough to stand up in peaks, 7 to 10 minutes. Remove from water; add vanilla extract. Beat until thick enough to spread.

*Enough to fill and frost a
9-inch 2-layer cake*

After Christmas in 1963, Chancellor Ludwig Erhard of Germany spent a weekend with the Lyndon B. Johnsons on their central Texas ranch. He was treated to Texas barbeques, fried catfish, and American pecan and apple pies. The dessert served at luncheon one day was a chocolate cake with a typically Texan coconut-pecan frosting.

Lyndon B. Johnson's

TEXAS CHOCOLATE CAKE

 4 ounces sweet chocolate
 ½ cup boiling water
 1 cup butter
 1 teaspoon vanilla extract
 2 cups sugar
 4 eggs, separated
2½ cups sifted cake flour
 1 teaspoon baking soda
 ½ teaspoon salt
 1 cup buttermilk
   Texas Coconut-Pecan Frosting (see recipe)

Melt chocolate in the boiling water; cool. Cream butter and vanilla extract thoroughly; add sugar gradually, creaming until fluffy after each addition. Add egg yolks, one at a time, and beat well after each addition. Mix in melted chocolate. Sift flour, baking soda, and salt together; add alternately in fourths with buttermilk to creamed mixture, beating well after each addition. Fold in egg whites, beaten until stiff, not dry, peaks are formed. Turn into three 8-inch greased (bottoms only) layer-cake pans. Bake at 350°F. 30 to 40 minutes, or until cake tests done. Cool layers completely before frosting with Texas Coconut-Pecan Frosting.

One 8-inch 3-layer cake

Texas Coconut-Pecan Frosting

 1 cup evaporated milk
 1 cup sugar
 3 egg yolks
 ½ cup butter or margarine
 1 teaspoon vanilla extract
1⅓ cups flaked coconut
 1 cup chopped pecans

Combine evaporated milk, sugar, egg yolks, butter and vanilla extract. Cook and stir over medium heat until thickened, about 12 minutes. Remove from heat. Add coconut and pecans. Beat until cool and thick enough to spread.

*Enough to frost tops of
three 8-inch round cake layers*

EASY BAKE DEVIL'S FOOD CAKE

    4 squares (4 ounces) unsweetened chocolate
    ½ cup butter
    1 cup water
    2 cups sifted cake flour
    2 cups sugar
    1½ teaspoons baking soda
    1 teaspoon salt
    2 eggs
    1 teaspoon vanilla extract
    ½ cup buttermilk
      Icing (see recipe)

Combine chocolate, butter, and water in a saucepan; place over low heat until chocolate is melted, stirring occasionally. Sift together into a large bowl the flour, sugar, baking soda, and salt. Beating well after each addition, add chocolate mixture to the dry ingredients, then the eggs, vanilla extract, and buttermilk. Turn into a greased and floured 13 x 9 x 2-inch baking pan; bake at 350°F. for 40 to 45 minutes, or until cake tests done. This recipe will make approximately 30 cupcakes. Cool and ice. *One 13 x 9-inch cake*

Icing

    1 stick (½ cup) butter, softened
    ⅛ teaspoon salt
    1 pound confectioners' sugar
    2 teaspoons vanilla extract
    ¼ cup milk

Put butter into a large bowl. Mix in salt, confectioners' sugar, vanilla extract, and milk. Beat at a high speed for a minute until all is well blended; spread over cake.

ORANGE BRUNCH CAKE

    1 cup butter, softened
    1 cup sugar
    2 egg yolks
    1 teaspoon vanilla extract
    1½ tablespoons grated orange peel
    2½ cups sifted all-purpose flour
    1 teaspoon baking powder
    1 teaspoon baking soda
    ¼ teaspoon salt
    1 cup buttermilk
    1 cup chopped nuts
    1 cup chopped dates
    2 egg whites
    ¼ teaspoon salt

Gradually add sugar to softened butter, beating until creamy. Add egg yolks, one at a time, beating until fluffy after each addition. Add vanilla extract and grated orange peel. Sift flour, baking powder, baking soda, and ¼ teaspoon salt together. Add alternately to egg mixture with buttermilk, beginning and ending with dry ingredients and beating until blended after each addition. Stir in a mixture of nuts and dates. Beat egg whites until frothy; add ¼ teaspoon salt and continue beating until stiff, not dry, peaks are formed. Fold into batter. Turn into a greased (bottom only) and floured 13 x 9 x 2-inch pan. Bake at 350°F. about 40 minutes, or until cake tests done. Pour this special sauce over the cake while still warm. (Don't omit this step . . . it's important to the flavor of the cake.) Combine 6 tablespoons **orange juice** and ½ cup **sugar.** Heat to boiling and pour over the cake.

One 13 x 9-inch cake

30TH PRESIDENT 1923-1929

Calvin Coolidge was born on Independence Day in 1872 in Plymouth, near Rutland, in the Vermont Mountains, at the back of his grandfather's general store in a five-room cottage, now maintained privately as a museum. The son of John and Victoria Moor Coolidge, he came from a long line of farmers and storekeepers.

Most outstanding diplomatic achievement of Coolidge's administration was the Kellogg-Briand Treaty of 1928, signed in Paris by a total of 62 nations, including Germany, Italy, and Japan. The pact outlawed war "as an instrument of national policy."

About a century ago, Election Day in New England was a great event with its own food traditions. After a trip to the polls, large groups met to celebrate victory or defeat. These Election Day guests were served a rich yeast cake, which originated in Hartford. This was always accompanied by punch or eggnog.

ELECTION DAY YEAST CAKE

½ cup warm water (105°-115°F.)
2 packages active dry yeast
½ cup milk, scalded and cooled to lukewarm
1½ cups sifted all-purpose flour
1¾ cups sifted all-purpose flour
1 teaspoon salt
1½ teaspoons ground cinnamon
½ teaspoon ground mace
½ teaspoon ground nutmeg
¼ teaspoon ground cloves
½ cup butter
¾ cup sugar
3 eggs, well beaten
1 cup pecans, chopped
3 oz. candied citron, chopped

Soften yeast in warm water in a bowl. Stir lukewarm milk into yeast. Add gradually the 1½ cups sifted flour, beating well after each addition. Beat until smooth. Cover bowl with waxed paper and a clean towel; let rise in a warm place (80°F.) until very light and bubbly, about 45 minutes. Meanwhile, sift together remaining flour, salt, and spices. Set aside. Cream butter until softened. Add sugar gradually, creaming until fluffy. Add beaten eggs in thirds, beating thoroughly after each addition. Blend in yeast mixture. Beating until smooth after each addi-

tion, gradually add dry ingredients. Mix in pecans and citron. Turn mixture into a greased (bottom only) 9-inch tubed pan. Cover with waxed paper and towel and let rise in a warm place away from drafts until pan is almost full, about 2 hours. Bake at 350°F. 50 to 55 minutes. Remove from oven to a wire rack and cool 10 minutes in pan. Cut around tube with a knife to loosen cake. Loosen sides with spatula; invert on wire rack and lift off pan. Cool cake completely before slicing.   *One 9-inch tubed cake*

The wedding of Alice Lee Roosevelt and Nicholas Longworth in 1906 was a most brilliant event in White House history.

Desserts

THE FACT THAT SUGAR was for so many years imported, scarce, and costly never restrained the popularity of desserts nor the proliferation of dessert recipes . . . from the provincialism of Bess Truman's Ozark Pudding to the sophistication of Jacqueline Kennedy's Gâteau Saint-Honoré, from "Whipt" Syllabub to Grasshopper Torte.

Research suggests that every visitor to the White House who ever met the First Lady asked for the President's favorite dessert recipe . . . and then published it in a cookbook. In no other area of the culinary arts is history so prolific, and the selection of these outstanding examples became an enjoyable exercise in taste testing and editorial judgment.

Lemon Pie was a favorite of Teddy Roosevelt.

LEMON PIE

    1½ cups sugar
    7 tablespoons cornstarch
    ¼ teaspoon salt
    ½ cup cold water
    1 cup boiling water
    3 egg yolks, slightly beaten
    2 tablespoons butter
    1 teaspoon grated lemon peel
    ½ cup lemon juice
      One baked 9-inch pastry shell
      Meringue (see recipe)

Thoroughly mix sugar, cornstarch, and salt in a heavy saucepan. Stir in the cold water. Add the boiling water gradually, stirring constantly. Bring mixture rapidly to boiling; reduce heat. Cook and stir about 10 minutes longer. Stir about ½ cup of the hot mixture into beaten egg yolks. Immediately blend into mixture in pan. Stir and cook over low heat 3 minutes. Blend in the next three ingredients. Cool. Turn filling into baked pastry shell. Top with meringue and bake at 350°F. 15 minutes, or until meringue is delicately browned. Cool on a wire rack until ready to serve.
One 9-inch pie

Meringue

    3 egg whites
    1 teaspoon lemon juice
    6 tablespoons sugar

Beat egg whites and lemon juice until frothy. Gradually add sugar, beating constantly until stiff peaks are formed. Pile lightly over pie filling, sealing meringue to pastry edge. Bake as directed. *Meringue for a 9-inch pie*

One of the important ingredients in this typically spring dessert is bread crumbs used in place of a two-crust pastry—the bread crumbs help to absorb excess liquid from watery rhubarb and strawberries.

SPRINGTIME DEEP DISH PIE

    2 cups strawberries
    3 cups rhubarb
    1½ cups sugar
    2 tablespoons cornstarch
      Pastry For a One-Crust Pie (page 95)
    ½ cup fine dry bread crumbs

Wash, hull, and cut large strawberries in half; wash and cut rhubarb into 1-inch pieces. Toss both in a mixture of the sugar and cornstarch. Prepare top crust from pastry. Put bread crumbs in a deep pie dish. Cover with the fruit mixture; top with the pastry and seal at edges. Cut gashes in pastry for escape of steam. Bake at 425°F. 40 to 50 minutes, or until pastry is lightly browned.
One deep dish pie

GOLDEN APRICOT MERINGUE-TOPPED PIE

    ½ lb. (about 1½ cups) dried apricots, cut in
      quarters
    2 tablespoons sugar
      Canned apricot nectar
    1 package (3 ounces) orange-flavored gelatin
    2 tablespoons sugar
    ¼ teaspoon salt
      One baked 9-inch pastry shell
      Three-Minute Meringue (see recipe)

Cook apricots in water to just cover in a covered saucepan, until tender, about 8 minutes. Stir in 2 tablespoons sugar until dissolved. Let stand 5 minutes. Drain and set aside. Measure cooking liquid and add enough apricot nectar to equal 1¾ cups; or use all apricot nectar. Heat 1 cup of the apricot juice to boiling; pour it over a mixture of the gelatin, remaining 2 tablespoons sugar, and salt in a bowl. Stir until gelatin is dissolved; then stir in remaining juice. Chill until slightly thicker than thick, unbeaten egg white. Stir in drained apricots and turn mixture into baked pie shell. Chill until set but not firm. Top with Three-Minute Meringue and sprinkle with toasted coconut, if desired. Chill until firm. Keep refrigerated until ready to serve.
One 9-inch pie

Three-Minute Meringue

    2 egg whites
    2 tablespoons water
    ½ cup sugar
    ¼ teaspoon salt
      Few drops almond or vanilla extract

Put first four ingredients in the top of a double boiler. Beat with a rotary or electric beater until thoroughly blended. Place over rapidly boiling water and continue beating 2 minutes. Remove from heat (keep over hot water) and beat vigorously until mixture stands in stiff, glossy peaks. Blend in a few drops of extract. (This meringue is excellent over any jellied pie.)
Meringue for a 9-inch pie

President Tyler called his favorite dessert Tyler's Pudding, but most desserts then were referred to as pudding. Today we call this recipe a coconut custard pie. If you shred fresh coconut, as the Tylers did, the recipe makes as rich and fresh a pie today as when Tyler enjoyed it.

President Tyler's
FAVORITE DESSERT

    4 eggs, slightly beaten
    ½ cup sugar
    ¼ teaspoon salt
    1½ cups milk, scalded
    ¾ cup heavy cream, scalded
    1 teaspoon vanilla extract
    1 cup shredded fresh coconut
    One unbaked 9-inch pastry shell

Add sugar and salt to eggs in a bowl and beat until just blended. Gently mix in the scalded milk and cream and vanilla extract. Strain mixture into a bowl; stir in coconut. Turn into pastry shell. Bake at 450°F. for 10 minutes. Reduce temperature to 350°F. and bake about 25 minutes longer, or until a silver knife inserted halfway between center and edge of filling comes out clean. Cool on a wire rack. Store in refrigerator until ready to serve.   *One 9-inch pie*

Abraham Lincoln was a sparse eater. If he had a favorite light repast it was apples. But the popular way to serve apples during the period corresponding with Lincoln's life, as it had been in George Washington's time, was apple pie, with a good coating of hot rum sauce.

Abraham Lincoln's
VIRGINIA GREEN APPLE PIE

    Pastry For a Two-Crust Pie (page 95)
    6 medium-sized tart green apples, pared, cored, and sliced
    1 cup sugar
    1 tablespoon cornstarch
    1 teaspoon ground cinnamon
    ½ teaspoon ground nutmeg
    ¼ teaspoon salt
    1 teaspoon lemon juice
    Butter pieces
    Hot Rum Sauce (see recipe)

Line a 9-inch pie pan with half the pastry. Roll out remainder for top crust; set aside. Arrange apple slices in pan. Combine sugar, cornstarch, cinnamon, nutmeg, and salt; sprinkle over apples. Drizzle with lemon juice and dot generously with butter pieces. Wet the rim of the pie crust with water. Cover with top crust; seal by fluting or crimping top and bottom crusts together. Cut gashes in upper crust for escape of steam. Bake pie at 425°F. for 15 minutes; reduce heat to 375°F. and bake 45 minutes. Before serving, spoon over the pie slices a little Hot Rum Sauce.   *One 9-inch pie*

Hot Rum Sauce

    ½ cup sugar
    1 tablespoon cornstarch
    ¼ teaspoon salt
    2 cups milk, scalded
    1 egg, slightly beaten
    1 teaspoon vanilla extract
    Rum

Mix dry ingredients in a small saucepan. Stir in scalded milk and bring rapidly to boiling; reduce heat. Cook, stirring constantly, until thickened and clear, about 3 minutes. Stir a little hot sauce into beaten egg; immediately return to pan, stirring constantly. Cook and stir over low heat 3 minutes. Add vanilla extract and rum to taste; serve hot.   *About 2 cups sauce*

LATTICE-TOP CHERRY PIE

    Pastry For a Two-Crust Pie (page 95)
    2 cans (16 ounces each) pitted red tart cherries*, drained (reserve ¾ cup liquid)
    ¾ to 1 cup sugar
    2½ tablespoons cornstarch
    ⅛ teaspoon salt
    1 teaspoon lemon juice
    ¼ teaspoon almond extract
    4 or 5 drops red food coloring
    1 tablespoon butter or margarine

Prepare pastry shell using ½ of the pastry; set aside. Blend sugar, cornstarch, and salt in a heavy saucepan. Gradually add the cherry liquid, mixing well. Bring rapidly to boiling and boil 2 to 3 minutes, stirring constantly. Remove from heat; stir in lemon juice, extract, and food coloring. Mix in the cherries. Set aside to cool. Roll out remaining pastry and cut into strips for the lattice top; set aside. When filling is cool, spoon into pastry shell. Dot with butter or margarine. Top with pastry strips to form a lattice design. Bake at 450°F. 10 minutes, or until pastry is lightly browned.   *One 8-inch pie*

*Water-packed cherries are preferred.

Lime Silk Pie is definitely a light party dessert. The lime flavor is enhanced by the addition of the aromatic herbs in the liqueur, chartreuse. Built upon a light meringue base, this pie is different, elegant, and as smooth as silk.

LIME SILK PIE

3 egg whites
¼ teaspoon salt
¼ teaspoon cream of tartar
¾ cup sugar
3 egg yolks
½ cup sugar
7 tablespoons lime juice
1 tablespoon chartreuse
   Few drops green food coloring
1 cup whipped cream
1 cup sweetened whipped cream
   Ground pistachio nuts

Beat egg whites, salt, and cream of tartar until frothy. Add the ¾ cup sugar a little at a time, beating thoroughly after each addition. Continue to beat until stiff peaks are formed. Spread meringue in a generously buttered 8-inch pie pan. Bake at 250°F. about 2 hours, or until meringue is well dried out and firm. Combine egg yolks and the ½ cup sugar in the top of a double boiler; beat until thick. Stir in lime juice. Cook slowly over hot (not boiling) water, stirring until mixture thickens, about 20 minutes. Remove from water and stir in chartreuse and a few drops of green food coloring. Cool. Fold in the 1 cup whipped cream. Pour into meringue shell and refrigerate until ready to use. Before serving, pile the top with the sweetened whipped cream and garnish with the nuts.   *One 8-inch pie*

It took a lot of rum in the old days to keep New England warm. Workers stopped for a rum break (the beginning of our coffee break?) mornings and afternoons. Housewives used rum for flavoring their cakes, breads, and pies. Rum pie, an egg custard flavored with rum and set in a pastry shell, was a colonial favorite. Today, melted marshmallows or cream cheese are also used as a base. This "down east" recipe makes two 8-inch pies.

DOWN EAST RUM PIE

1½ cups crushed vanilla wafers
½ cup crushed gingersnaps
½ cup sugar
¾ cup butter
4 packages (3 ounces each) cream cheese, softened
½ cup packed brown sugar
¼ teaspoon salt
3 eggs, well beaten
1 cup heavy cream
4 tablespoons rum
4 tablespoons chocolate decorettes or shavings

Mix crushed vanilla wafers, gingersnaps, and sugar. Blend in butter using a pastry blender or two knives. Press mixture firmly on the bottoms and sides of two 8-inch pie pans. Chill while preparing filling. Beat cream cheese, brown sugar, and salt until smooth. Gradually beat in eggs, cream, and rum. Pour into chilled crusts. Bake at 275°F. about 40 minutes, or until set. Remove from oven and sprinkle with chocolate decorettes or shavings. Chill pies until ready to serve. Serve very cold.   *Two 8-inch pies*

Herbert Clark Hoover was born at West Branch, Iowa, Aug. 10, 1874. His youth was spent mostly at Salem, Ore., where he attended public schools before entering Stanford University as a student of mining engineering. He was graduated in 1895.

31ST PRESIDENT

1929-1933

In Europe in World War I, Hoover organized the American Relief Committee, later headed the Commission for Relief in Belgium.

Mrs. Roosevelt's Pecan Pie is delicious but not as rich as Mrs. Lyndon Johnson's Pecan Pie. Many people might prefer this less rich version.

Mrs. F. D. Roosevelt's

PECAN PIE

1 tablespoon butter
1 cup packed brown sugar
1 cup corn syrup
3 eggs, well beaten
1 teaspoon vanilla extract
Few grains salt
1 cup pecan halves
One unbaked 9-inch pastry shell

Blend butter and brown sugar. Beat in corn syrup, eggs, vanilla extract, and salt until thoroughly blended. Stir in nuts. Turn into pie shell and bake at 375°F. until firm.   *One 9-inch pie*

Lady Bird Johnson's

PECAN PIE

½ cup butter
1 cup sugar
1 cup dark corn syrup
1½ teaspoons vanilla extract
½ teaspoon salt
3 eggs, well beaten
2 cups pecans, coarsely chopped
One unbaked 9-inch pastry shell

Let butter stand at room temperature in a covered mixing bowl until very soft. Add sugar, corn syrup, vanilla extract, and salt; beat until thoroughly blended. Add eggs and beat gently until blended. Stir in pecans. Pour into pie shell and bake at 375°F. about 40 minutes, or until top is toasted brown and filling is set when the pie is gently rocked.   *One 9-inch pie*

PUMPKIN PIE

2 cups (16-ounce can) canned pumpkin
⅔ cup packed brown sugar
1 teaspoon ground cinnamon
½ teaspoon ground ginger
½ teaspoon ground nutmeg
⅛ teaspoon ground cloves
½ teaspoon salt
2 eggs, slightly beaten
2 cups cream, scalded
One unbaked 9-inch pastry shell

Mix together pumpkin and brown sugar in a bowl. Stir in a mixture of spices and salt. Mix in the eggs. Gradually add cream, stirring until mixture is smooth. Turn into the pastry shell. Bake at 400°F. about 50 minutes, or until a silver knife comes out clean when inserted halfway between center and edge. Cool on wire rack. Serve warm or cold with **sweetened whipped cream** or top with **Crunchy Coated Pecans** (see recipe).   *One 9-inch pie*

Crunchy Coated Pecans

3 tablespoons butter
1 cup pecan halves
¼ cup packed brown sugar

Melt butter in a small skillet over low heat. Add pecans. Occasionally turn pecans until thoroughly coated with butter. Turn nuts into a bowl containing the brown sugar and toss to coat thoroughly. When pie is cool, arrange coated pecans, rounded side up, over top of pie in an attractive design. Place under broiler about 3 inches from source of heat. Broil 1 to 2 minutes. Serve pie warm or cold with **sweetened whipped cream.**

Mrs. Grace Coolidge's

BUTTERSCOTCH PIE

2 tablespoons butter
1 cup packed brown sugar
1 cup milk
2 tablespoons all-purpose flour
1 teaspoon cornstarch
½ teaspoon salt
2 eggs, separated
1 teaspoon vanilla extract
One baked 7-inch pastry shell

Heat butter, sugar, and ½ cup of the milk in a saucepan over medium heat; stir until sugar is dissolved. Blend remaining ½ cup milk into a mixture of flour, cornstarch, and salt in a small bowl. Add to sugar mixture, stirring constantly. Bring rapidly to boiling; reduce heat and cook, stirring, until thickened and clear. Beat egg yolks with a fork; add about ½ cup of the hot mixture, stirring until blended. Immediately return to mixture in pan; cook and stir 1 minute longer. Cool, then fold in vanilla extract and egg whites beaten until stiff, not dry, peaks are formed. Turn into baked pie shell. Top with whipped cream, if desired.   *One 7-inch pie*

President Benjamin Harrison, "the log-cabin candidate," was born and educated on this farm in North Bend, Ohio.

Calvin Coolidge was very particular that the White House staff use only Mrs. Coolidge's recipes when making corn muffins and custard pie, two Coolidge favorites. Here is the recipe for her famous custard pie, also her butterscotch.

Mrs. Grace Coolidge's

CUSTARD PIE

- ¾ cup sugar
- 1 tablespoon flour
  Pinch salt
- 2 eggs, slightly beaten
- ¾ teaspoon vanilla extract
- 2½ cups milk, scalded
  One unbaked 7-inch pastry shell

Mix sugar, flour, and salt in a bowl. Blend in eggs and vanilla extract. Slowly add the milk, stirring constantly. Pour into pie shell and bake at 400°F. 25 to 30 minutes. Dust a little nutmeg on top after pie is baked. Cool on wire rack before cutting. *One 7-inch pie*

PASTRY FOR A ONE-CRUST PIE

- 1 cup sifted all-purpose flour
- ¼ teaspoon salt
- 6 tablespoons shortening
- 3 tablespoons water

Sift together flour and salt; cut in shortening with pastry blender or two knives. Add water; mix into dry ingredients with pastry blender.

Gather pastry together and shape into a ball. Turn dough onto a lightly floured pastry canvas. Bring ends of pastry canvas together; press dough into a ball. Unfold canvas and shape dough into a patty; roll it 1 inch larger than inverted pie pan. Fold dough into quarters and gently place in pie pan. Unfold and gently ease pastry to fit pie pan without pulling or stretching dough. Trim and flute edge. Prick bottom and sides with a fork. Bake at 425°F. 18 to 20 minutes or until pastry is a delicate brown.

One 7- or 8-inch baked pastry shell

PASTRY FOR A TWO-CRUST PIE

- 3 cups sifted all-purpose flour
- 1 teaspoon salt
- 1 cup lard or other shortening
- 5 tablespoons cold water

Sift the flour and salt together. Cut in the lard with pastry blender or two knives until pieces are the size of small peas. Gradually sprinkle water over mixture, mixing lightly with a fork after each addition; add only enough water to hold pastry together. Roll out on a floured surface and fit into pie pan. Don't stretch pastry when fitting into pan, as this will cause shrinkage in finished product. Use as directed in pie recipes. *Enough for two or three 1-crust pies or one 2-crust pie*

NOTE: Any pastry left from shaping pies may be cut in fancy shapes or sticks, sprinkled with cinnamon and sugar, and baked for nibblers.

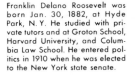

Franklin Delano Roosevelt was born Jan. 30, 1882, at Hyde Park, N. Y. He studied with private tutors and at Groton School, Harvard University, and Columbia Law School. He entered politics in 1910 when he was elected to the New York state senate.

32ND PRESIDENT

1933-1945

Two months before his sudden death in April, 1945, Roosevelt met at Yalta with Churchill and Stalin to negotiate postwar arrangements.

Serve this light dessert in the spring when juicy Louisiana strawberries are plentiful.

STRAWBERRIES LOUISIENNE

1 quart strawberries
3 tablespoons confectioners' sugar
3 tablespoons sherry
1 cup heavy cream
   Confectioners' sugar
   Grated orange peel

This easy dessert is done in two steps. In the morning, or sometime before serving, wash and hull strawberries; place in a bowl and sprinkle with the 3 tablespoons confectioners' sugar and the sherry. Reserve 5 or 6 strawberries. Cover bowl and refrigerate until ready to serve. Puree reserved berries through a sieve into a cup. Cover and refrigerate. Just before serving, beat cream until it stands in peaks, adding enough confectioners' sugar to sweeten to taste. Fold in the pureed strawberries for a delicate pink color. Spoon whole berries into sherbets with a little of the juice drawn from them; top with dollops of the pink whipped cream. Garnish the top of each with a sprinkling of grated orange peel.

About 6 servings

Strawberries are also delicious when subtly marinated in Arrack. Arrack is a liquor widely favored in the days of Washington and Jefferson, but little known today. Strawberries in Arrack are equally good when used as a "starter" for a meal.

STRAWBERRIES IN ARRACK

7 tablespoons water
7 tablespoons sugar
1 pint strawberries
½ cup Rose's lime juice
½ teaspoon Arrack

Mix water and sugar in a saucepan. Cover, bring to boiling and boil 2 to 3 minutes. Cool. Wash, hull, and slice strawberries. When syrup is cool, add lime juice and Arrack. The flavor should be subtle, not strong. Place strawberries in marinade and chill thoroughly until used.

4 servings

Teddy Roosevelt's BAKED APPLES

8 tart apples
½ cup sugar
¼ teaspoon ground cinnamon
   Pinch of ground allspice

Remove blossom end from apples, then remove core being careful not to cut through the bottom; do not pare. Mix sugar, cinnamon, and allspice. Fill cavities in apples. If desired, dot with butter. Set in a little boiling water in a baking pan. Bake at 450°F. 20 to 30 minutes. Serve in the syrup.

8 servings

The Kennedy version of stewed fruit is both eye appealing and nutritious. The addition of a sour cream topping elevates the fruit to a nice luncheon dessert, or a possible addition to the kaffeeklatsch.

John F. Kennedy's
HOT FRUIT DESSERT

1 orange
1 lemon
3 tablespoons light brown sugar
1 can (8¾ ounces) apricot halves, drained
1 can (8¾ ounces) pineapple tidbits, drained
1 can (8¾ ounces) peach slices, drained
1 can (8¾ ounces) pitted dark, sweet cherries, drained
Freshly grated nutmeg
Dairy sour cream

Grate peel of orange and lemon. Mix grated peel with brown sugar. Pare orange and lemon and slice very thin. Arrange in a 1-quart baking dish in alternate layers with drained canned fruits. Sprinkle each layer with some of the brown sugar mixture and a sprinkling of nutmeg. Heat in a 375°F. oven until very hot. Serve topped with sour cream.   *About 6 servings*

NOTE: For a larger quantity, double or triple recipe, as desired.

Richard M. Nixon's
CRUSTLESS APPLE PIE

⅓ to ½ cup granulated sugar
1 teaspoon ground cinnamon
1 cup water
6 medium (about 2 pounds) cooking apples, washed, cut in eighths, cored, and pared
1 cup sifted all-purpose flour
1 teaspoon baking powder
Salt, if desired
6 tablespoons shortening
½ cup firmly packed brown sugar

Blend granulated sugar and cinnamon in a large heavy saucepan. Stir in water and apples. Bring to boiling, reduce heat, and cook 10 minutes, stirring occasionally. Meanwhile, sift flour, baking powder, and salt (if used) together; blend thoroughly and set aside. Put shortening into a mixing bowl and cream it with the brown sugar. Beat in the flour mixture, adding gradually. Turn apples and syrup into a greased 9-inch pie pan. Cover apples completely with the topping. Bake at 350°F. about 35 minutes, or until apples are tender and topping is browned. Set on wire rack. Serve hot or cold with whipped cream, if desired.   *One 9-inch pie*

The staff at the Hermitage, Andrew Jackson's Tennessee estate, obviously didn't use the double boiler we use today. We have rephrased the old receipt for convenience's sake. The double boilers of old were called "bain maries," and the housewife who did not have one would set a kettle of water to boiling, fill a deep china dish with custard, set the dish in the boiling water, and take a hot iron from the fire to color the custard at the top. Custards were usually flavored with rose water or scrapings from a vanilla bean. This soft custard recipe is from The Hermitage.

Andrew Jackson's
BEST "BOILED" CUSTARD

1 quart milk, scalded
4 eggs
1 cup sugar
2 teaspoons vanilla extract or sherry

Beat eggs, gradually adding sugar. (In olden days the sugar was very coarse, compared to the granulated sugar of today, and it was necessary to sift it.) Slowly add some of the scalded milk to egg mixture, stirring constantly. Add to milk in double boiler; place over simmering water. Cook, stirring, until mixture coats a spoon. Remove from water and place in cold water to cool, stirring occasionally. Add extract or sherry to custard. Serve very cold with sponge cake and a spoon of "whipt" cream, if desired.   *8 servings*

A Currier and Ives print of a family celebration of Thanksgiving Day, 1867, portraying the significance of America's best loved holiday.

This is a very old recipe, given to the second Mrs. Theodore Roosevelt by her grandmother. Though simple and homespun, it is still a delicate pudding. Old recipes are invariably large in their quantities; this one serves 16 people generously.

Mrs. Teddy Roosevelt's
INDIAN PUDDING

3 pints milk
7 tablespoons yellow cornmeal
5 eggs, well beaten
½ cup dark molasses
1 cup raisins
½ cup butter
½ cup packed dark brown sugar
1 teaspoon salt
½ teaspoon ground cinnamon
½ teaspoon ground ginger
½ teaspoon ground nutmeg
1 cup cold milk

Scald the 3 pints milk in the top of a double boiler over low heat (in the very early days they used a bain marie for this purpose). Place over boiling water and add cornmeal a little at a time, stirring until blended. Cook 15 minutes, stirring occasionally. Vigorously stir about 3 tablespoons of the hot mixture into a mixture of the beaten eggs and molasses. Blend into the hot cornmeal mixture. Stir in raisins, butter, sugar, salt, and spices. Turn into a buttered 4-quart baking dish. Pour over top the 1 cup cold milk. (Do not stir milk in.) Bake at 300°F. about 2 hours, or until top is browned. Serve with **cream, sweetened whipped cream, ice cream,** or **Hot Rum Sauce** (page 92). *16 servings*

For smaller families, here is another Indian Pudding.

INDIAN PUDDING

3 cups milk
½ cup yellow cornmeal
¼ cup sugar
1 teaspoon salt
1 teaspoon ground cinnamon
½ teaspoon ground ginger
1 egg, well beaten
½ cup light molasses
2 tablespoons butter
1 cup cold milk

Scald the 3 cups milk in the top of a double boiler over simmering water. Stirring constantly, slowly blend scalded milk into a mixture of the cornmeal, sugar, salt, cinnamon, and ginger. Vigorously stir some of the hot mixture into a blend of beaten egg and molasses. Stir into hot cornmeal mixture. Cook over boiling water until very thick, about 10 minutes; stir constantly. Beat in the butter. Turn mixture into a generously buttered 1½-qt. casserole. Pour cold milk over top. Bake at 300°F. for 2 hours, or until browned. Serve warm with **heavy cream** or **ice cream.** *About 6 servings*

Mrs. F. D. Roosevelt's
CHOCOLATE SOUFFLE

2 teaspoons butter
2 teaspoons flour
¾ cup milk
1½ squares (1½ ounces) unsweetened chocolate, melted
⅓ cup sugar
2 teaspoons hot water
3 eggs, separated
½ teaspoon vanilla extract
Mrs. Roosevelt's Cream Sauce (see recipe)

Melt butter in a saucepan; blend in flour and gradually add milk, stirring constantly. Bring to boiling; cook 2 minutes. Remove from heat. Blend melted chocolate, sugar, and hot water. Stir until smooth. Stir into milk mixture, blending thoroughly. Beat egg yolks until thick and lemon colored. Slowly add chocolate-milk mixture and beat until blended. Fold in egg whites beaten until stiff, not dry, peaks are formed and vanilla extract. Turn into a buttered 1½-quart soufflé dish (straight-sided casserole) and bake at 350°F. 25 minutes, or until a knife inserted halfway between center and edge comes out clean. Serve immediately with Mrs. Roosevelt's Cream Sauce. *About 4 servings*

Mrs. F. D. Roosevelt's
CREAM SAUCE

¾ cup heavy cream
½ cup milk
⅓ cup confectioners' sugar
1 teaspoon vanilla extract

Mix cream and milk in a chilled bowl. Beat with chilled beaters until thick. Blend in confectioners' sugar and vanilla extract.
About 1½ cups sauce

This is the recipe for FDR's favorite chocolate pudding. The recipe originally came from Rhode Island.

Franklin D. Roosevelt's
MACAROON CHOCOLATE CREAM

    3 eggs
    ⅓ cup sugar
    2 tablespoons Dutch process cocoa
    2½ cups milk, scalded
    8 macaroons, finely rolled
    2 tablespoons chopped almonds
      Whipped cream

Beat eggs and sugar until thick and light in color in the top of a double boiler. Stir in cocoa. When cocoa is dissolved, pour in scalded milk. Cook over simmering water until very thick, stirring all the time. Remove from water; mix in crushed macaroons and almonds. Chill thoroughly. Serve with small spoonfuls of **whipped cream** floating on top.   *6 servings*

It is said that the original recipe for Crème Brûlée was introduced to America in the collection of French recipes that Thomas Jefferson brought back with him in 1790. Whatever the source, it is an elegant and toothsome dessert . . . and a special favorite of Jacqueline Kennedy.

Jacqueline Kennedy's
CREME BRULEE

    3 cups heavy cream
    1-inch piece vanilla bean
    6 egg yolks
    6 tablespoons sugar
    ½ cup brown sugar

In the upper part of a double boiler, heat heavy cream with the piece of vanilla bean. In a bowl, beat egg yolks with sugar until light and creamy. Take out the vanilla bean and stir the warm cream into yolks very carefully and slowly. Return the mixture to the double boiler; cook over hot water, stirring constantly, until the custard coats the spoon. Then put into a glass serving dish and place it in the refrigerator to set. When ready to serve, cover the top of the custard completely with brown sugar, using ½ cup or more. Place the dish on a bowl of crushed ice and place custard under broiler flame until sugar melts and caramelizes. Keep watching it, for the sugar will burn. Serve immediately. (This recipe from the White House calls for the Crème Brûlée to be served warm. Traditional preparation calls for the Brûlée to be chilled in the refrigerator several hours. They are just as tasty served cold and might be somewhat easier to handle.)   *8 servings*

Harry S. Truman was born in Lamar, Mo., May 8, 1884. He began his schooling in Independence, Mo., at the age of 9 and at 17 became a bookkeeper at a Kansas City bank. At 22 he returned to the family farm, where he remained until he joined the Army as a lieutenant in the artillery in 1917.

33RD PRESIDENT

1945-1953

Truman became President upon Franklin D. Roosevelt's death in April, 1945. After Germany's surrender, he met with Attlee and Stalin at Potsdam.

A gourmet dessert topped with a glaze of delicious Bing cherries from the home state of a gourmet President, Martin Van Buren.

CHEESECAKE, VAN BUREN

1½ cups crushed zwieback
2 tablespoons brown sugar
¼ cup melted butter
2 packages (8 ounces each) cream cheese, softened
1 cup sugar
6 eggs, separated
2 tablespoons flour
  Pinch salt
1 teaspoon grated lemon peel
1 tablespoon lemon juice
  New York Glaze (see recipe)

Blend zwieback crumbs, brown sugar, and butter. Line the bottom and sides of a generously buttered 10-inch springform pan with a thin layer of crumb mixture; press firmly. Beat cream cheese and sugar until fluffy. Beat in egg yolks one at a time. Stir in flour, salt, lemon peel and juice. Beat egg whites until stiff, not dry, peaks are formed. Fold into cream cheese mixture. Turn into prepared pan. Bake at 350°F. until center tests done, about 1 to 1½ hours. Remove to wire rack to cool completely. When cooled, pour glaze over cheesecake and refrigerate until glaze is set.

One 10-inch cheesecake

New York Glaze

1 jar (17 ounces) pitted dark sweet cherries in heavy syrup
2 tablespoons sugar
1½ teaspoons cornstarch
⅛ teaspoon salt
½ cup water
1 teaspoon brandy
1 teaspoon Madeira

Drain cherries, reserving ¼ cup syrup. Combine sugar, cornstarch, and salt in a small saucepan. Add gradually, stirring constantly, a mixture of the reserved syrup and water. Bring rapidly to boiling and cook, stirring, about 3 min., or until mixture is thickened and clear. Remove from heat; stir in brandy, Madeira, and a few drops of red food coloring if desired. Add cherries and pour over cooled cheesecake. Place in the refrigerator until glaze is set.

At President Jackson's Hermitage estate, there is an old manuscript cookbook of the Jacksons.

One of his favorite desserts was English Trifle made with macaroons, sherry or sack, and orange marmalade. Trifle was also a favorite of the Washingtons, especially Martha. It is an elegant dessert, attested to by the fact that early recipes started out "Take your best cut glass bowl . . . ". Although cut glass isn't necessary, if you do have a crystal bowl, use it. The dessert is especially attractive prepared this way. The following recipe was designed to fill a 2-quart bowl, about 9 inches in diameter.

ENGLISH TRIFLE

  Ladyfingers or sponge cake
4 tablespoons Madeira or sweet sherry (about)
  Raspberry jam
  Almond-flavored macaroons
2 cups milk
6 egg yolks
½ cup sugar
  Pinch salt
½ teaspoon vanilla extract
2 tablespoons brandy (optional)
1 teaspoon unflavored gelatin
1 tablespoon sugar
2 tablespoons water
1 cup heavy cream
  Split, blanched almonds

Line bottom of a cut glass or deep crystal bowl with ladyfingers or day-old sponge cake. Sprinkle just enough Madeira or sherry over ladyfingers or sponge cake to lightly moisten them. Spread a thin layer of jam on ladyfingers or sponge cake. Sprinkle coarsely broken macaroons over jam. Set aside in refrigerator. Scald milk. Lightly beat egg yolks in the top of a double boiler. Blend in the ½ cup sugar and salt. Slowly pour hot milk into egg mixture, stirring constantly. Place over hot water and cook, stirring constantly, until mixture coats a spoon. Remove from water and stir in vanilla extract and brandy, if used. Pour custard over ladyfinger mixture and chill overnight. Soften gelatin and dissolve remaining tablespoon sugar in the 2 tablespoons water. Place over hot water until gelatin is completely dissolved. Stir gelatin into cream and whip until mixture stands in peaks when beater is slowly lifted upright. Remove custard from refrigerator and sprinkle with almonds. Spread whipped cream over the top and refrigerate until topping becomes firm. Garnish and decorate with **glacé cherries, angelica,** or **sugar decorettes** named so succinctly by the English as "hundreds 'n' thousands."

About 8 servings

It was during Madison's administration that steamboats began traveling on the Mississippi, providing upriver transportation and strengthening the ties between the eastern and western sections of the country.

In the handed-down manuscript cookbook of Woodrow Wilson's mother, there is an annotation beside her handwritten recipe for Charlotte Russe, "Woodrow's favorite." The recipe is basically a Bavarian cream with a "churned" syllabub added. Today, Charlotte Russe is a Bavarian cream molded with ladyfingers and flavored with pureed fruits, chocolate, coffee, and sometimes liquor.

KENTUCKY CHARLOTTE RUSSE

¾ tablespoon unflavored gelatin
⅓ cup cold water
⅓ cup milk, scalded
⅓ cup confectioners' sugar
1½ teaspoons vanilla extract
1 tablespoon bourbon whiskey
1 cup heavy cream
Ladyfingers

Soak gelatin in the cold water in a bowl. Pour in scalded milk and stir until gelatin is dissolved. Set bowl in a pan of ice water and beat in sugar until mixture is fluffy. Stir in vanilla extract and bourbon. Beat in ⅓ cup of the heavy cream. Beat the remaining ⅔ cup cream until it stands in peaks when beater is slowly lifted upright. Fold into gelatin mixture. Line the bottom and sides of a 1-quart mold with ladyfingers. Turn gelatin mixture into mold. Chill until firm. Unmold onto a serving plate and garnish with additional **whipped cream.** Charlotte Russe may be made in individual molds also. *6 servings*

Jacqueline Kennedy's
CHILLED CHOCOLATE MOUSSE

2 squares (2 ounces) unsweetened chocolate, melted
½ cup confectioners' sugar
1 cup milk, scalded
¾ cup sugar
1 envelope unflavored gelatin
¼ teaspoon salt
½ cup water
1 teaspoon vanilla extract
2 cups heavy cream, whipped

Combine chocolate and confectioners' sugar in a saucepan. Gradually add scalded milk, stirring constantly. Place over low heat and stir until mixture almost reaches boiling point, but do not let boil. Remove from heat. Mix sugar, gelatin, and salt in a small saucepan. Stir in water and place over low heat until gelatin is dissolved, stirring constantly. Add gelatin mixture and vanilla extract to chocolate mixture. Chill until slightly thickened. Beat with a rotary beater until light and fluffy. Fold in whipped cream. Turn into a 2-quart mold or serving dish. Chill 2 to 3 hours. *6 to 8 servings*

Mrs. William Howard Taft's Dessert is a mocha-flavored version of the ancient, standard jelly roll recipe, sometimes referred to as Lincoln's Log. And, as in most old recipes, though the ingredients are there, the instructions are usually meager. In the older days of large families, even moderate-income families were able to have a hired cook. Maybe the cook was supposed to know what to do. Anyway, we'll give you Mrs. Taft's recipe with a few hints which we hope will make this a successful, as well as an authentic dessert.

Mrs. William Howard Taft's
DESSERT

- **6 egg yolks**
- **1 cup confectioners' sugar**
- **1 teaspoon vanilla extract**
- **1 teaspoon strong coffee**
- **1 cup sifted cake flour**
- **2 teaspoons cocoa**
- **1 teaspoon baking powder**
- **6 egg whites**
- **¼ teaspoon salt**
- **1 cup heavy cream, whipped**
- **1 teaspoon vanilla extract**
- **Rum Chocolate Icing (see recipe)**

Beat egg yolks until thick and light-colored. Gradually add the sugar, beating until mixture is very thick and creamy. Mix in 1 teaspoon vanilla extract and coffee. Sift flour, cocoa, and baking powder together. Gradually add to egg mixture, beating just until smooth after each addition. Add salt to egg whites and beat until stiff, not dry, peaks are formed. Fold into cake batter. Line a greased 15 x 10-inch jelly roll pan with waxed paper and grease again. Turn batter into pan spreading evenly to edges. Bake at 375°F. 12 to 13 minutes, or until cake springs back when lightly touched in center with finger. Loosen sides and turn cake out on a towel sprinkled with **confectioners' sugar.** Remove waxed paper and trim off hard crust. Cover cake with fresh waxed paper and roll cake while hot. Using towel as guide, begin rolling at narrow end of cake. Grasp edge of towel and pull it over beyond opposite edge; cake will roll itself as you pull. Wrap roll in towel and cool on wire rack. Blend the remaining teaspoon vanilla extract into whipped cream. When cake is cool, unroll, remove paper, and spread cake with cream mixture. Reroll. Spread with Rum Chocolate Icing. Garnish with stripes of **whipped cream** at the ends. *One cake roll*

Rum Chocolate Icing

- **4 squares (4 ounces) unsweetened chocolate**
- **¾ cup evaporated milk**
- **2 cups sugar**
- **¼ teaspoon salt**
- **2 tablespoons butter**
- **½ teaspoon vanilla extract**
- **2 to 4 tablespoons rum**

Melt chocolate in a heavy saucepan. Stir in milk, sugar, salt, and butter. Bring slowly to boiling. Remove from heat and beat until smooth. Add extract and rum to taste. Cool until of spreading consistency. *About 2 cups icing*

Dwight David Eisenhower was born in this frame house at Denison, Tex. Later his family moved to Abilene, Kan. There Dwight and his brothers attended school until he entered the United States Military Academy in 1911.

34TH PRESIDENT

1953-1961

President Eisenhower attended the Summit Conference at Geneva, July 18-23, 1955, with heads of state of France, Great Britain, and U.S.S.R. A victim of a heart attack two months later, he recovered to win reelection in 1956.

GRASSHOPPER TORTE

5 teaspoons unflavored gelatin
½ cup cold water
⅔ cup white crème de cocoa
⅓ cup green crème de menthe
2 cups heavy cream
1 orange chiffon or plain tubed angel food cake

Soften gelatin in the water. Set over hot water until gelatin is dissolved. Stir in the crème de cocoa and crème de menthe. Cool. Whip cream until it is fluffy but does not stand in peaks. Continuing to beat, slowly pour the gelatin mixture in a thin stream into cream. Beat until mixture stands in peaks when beater is slowly lifted upright. With a thread held taut between your hands (or with an electric knife), draw thread horizontally through the cake to make 5 narrow layers, as for a torte. Spread layers with filling and stack. Generously frost the top of the cake. Chill before serving.   *10 to 12 servings*

A different and simple fruit pastry dessert.

BAKED STUFFED PEAR DUMPLINGS

8 canned pear halves (29-ounce can),
     drained; reserve 1½ cups syrup for sauce
1 package (3 ounces) cream cheese, softened
Pastry For a Two-Crust Pie (page 95)
Spicy Sauce (see recipe)

Stuff pear halves with cream cheese. Set aside. Roll pastry into a large square about 15 x 15 inches. Using a pastry wheel for a fluted edge or a knife, cut eight strips about 1¾ inches wide. Moisten the lengthwise edge of each strip and wrap it around a pear half, overlapping the moist edges slightly so that the pear is completely sealed in a pastry blanket. Place on a lightly greased baking sheet or shallow pan and bake at 425°F. 30 to 35 minutes, or until pastry is a delicate golden brown. Serve dumplings warm in dessert dishes with Spicy Sauce poured over them.   *8 servings*

Spicy Sauce

6 tablespoons sugar
2 tablespoons cornstarch
¼ teaspoon salt
1½ cups pear syrup
1 tablespoon lemon juice
2 teaspoons butter
1½ tablespoons minced candied ginger

Mix the first three ingredients in a small saucepan. Add pear syrup gradually, stirring constantly. Bring rapidly to boiling and cook, stirring, about 3 minutes, or until mixture is thickened and clear. Stir in lemon juice, butter, and ginger. For those who like to cook with wines and liqueurs, a tablespoon of brandy, added at the last, is a gourmet touch.
          About 1⅔ cups sauce

Above is the re-creation of the kitchen at Mt. Vernon, where savory dishes were prepared from the heirloom recipes of Martha Washington's justly famous and quaint "Custis cookbook."

An easy dessert to prepare and a favorite with the children is Peppermint Whip. It has a nice color and a crunchy texture, which add to its deliciousness.

FROZEN PEPPERMINT WHIP

Vanilla wafers, crushed
1 cup heavy cream, whipped
1 cup miniature marshmallows
2 tablespoons chocolate decorettes
3 peppermint candy sticks (penny variety),
     crushed

Line bottom of a refrigerator tray with crushed vanilla wafers. Fold marshmallows, chocolate decorettes, and peppermint candy into whipped cream. Turn mixture into prepared tray and cover top with additional crushed wafers. Freeze until firm.   *About 6 servings*

Admittedly, Mamie Eisenhower doesn't care for cooking. Ike was the chef of the family. But Mamie made a "courtin" fudge she used to serve Ike when he was a young lieutenant. Legend has it that Ike gave it the name "Mamie's Million Dollar Fudge."

Mamie's
MILLION DOLLAR FUDGE

    4½ cups sugar
        Pinch salt
    2 tablespoons butter
    1 can (14½ oz.) evaporated milk
    12 ounces (1 package) semisweet
        chocolate pieces
    12 ounces sweet chocolate
    1 pint marshmallow cream
    2 cups nuts

Combine the first 4 ingredients and boil 6 minutes. Put the following into a large bowl: the chocolate pieces, the sweet chocolate, marshmallow cream, and nuts. Pour the boiling syrup over ingredients in the bowl; beat until chocolate is melted. Pour into pan; let stand a few hours before cutting. Store in tin box.

About 5 pounds candy

President Johnson's favorite candy recipe is given out as the family cook's recipe for Double Divinity Fudge. . . . and good, too, but a great deal more creamy than ordinary divinity.

President L. B. Johnson's
DOUBLE DIVINITY FUDGE

    2 cups sugar
    ⅔ cup water
    ½ cup light corn syrup
    2 egg whites
        Pinch salt
    1 teaspoon vanilla extract

Combine ½ cup sugar with ⅓ cup water, and cook to 240°F. (on candy thermometer) until small amount of syrup forms soft ball in cold water. Cook remaining 1½ cups sugar, ⅓ cup water, and corn syrup to 254°F. until it forms a hard ball in cold water. Cool first syrup slightly. Beat egg whites and salt until stiff, not dry, peaks are formed. Add first syrup slowly to egg whites, beating constantly until mixture loses its gloss, about 12 minutes; add second syrup in same way. Add vanilla extract and turn into buttered pan. Cut into squares when cold. *1 pound candy*

Marine Captain Charles Robb, and his bride, the former Lynda Johnson, walk through an arch of drawn swords as they leave the East Room of the White House December 9, 1967, following the wedding ceremony.

Jacqueline Kennedy loves gooey desserts, and here is one of her Frenchiest classics, Gâteau Saint-Honoré. The base of this confection is a pie dough; then a ¾-inch high ring of puff paste is forced around the edge of the circle. The center is filled with a crème pâtissière called Saint-Honoré. Individual cream puffs, somewhere between the size of a nickel and a quarter, are then made and filled with some of the pâtissière. Then an amber toffee syrup is made. The small, filled cream puffs are dipped in the syrup and then arranged around the creamy puff paste edging the cake. Top each cream puff with half of a candied cherry. Then the cake is finished with whipped cream swirls forced through a pastry tube. We have taken the liberty of rewriting, partly, the White House recipe in the hopes of making it easier to follow. Although the end result is ambrosial, we recommend this recipe only to the most experienced cook.

Jacqueline Kennedy's
GÂTEAU SAINT-HONORÉ

Base:
- ½ cup plus 2 tablespoons all-purpose flour
- Pinch salt
- 6 tablespoons shortening
- 5 tablespoons water

Mix salt and flour in a bowl. With fingers, crumble in shortening. Add water and mix just enough to form a tender dough, but do not work dough. Place in refrigerator ½ hour. Roll out into a circle 9 inches in diameter. Prick with the tines of a fork and place on a baking sheet.

Cream puffs:
- 1 cup hot water
- ½ cup butter
- 1 tablespoon sugar
- ½ teaspoon salt
- 1 cup sifted all-purpose flour
- 4 eggs

Bring water, butter, sugar, and salt to a rolling boil. Add flour all at once. Beat vigorously with a wooden spoon until mixture leaves sides of pan and forms a smooth ball. Remove from heat. Quickly beat in eggs, one at a time, beating until smooth after each addition. Continue beating until mixture is thick and smooth. Place mixture in pastry bag. Wet the edge of the pastry base and, using the pastry bag, pipe a ring ¾-inch high of puff paste around the edge of the pastry circle. Brush with fork-beaten **egg**. Place in a

400°F. oven **not below the center of the oven,** as the base bakes faster than the puff. Bake 10 minutes; then lower temperature to 350°F. and bake until puff paste is crisp and stands up. Cool on a wire rack. With the remainder of the puff paste, squeeze drops just a little larger than a nickel onto a greased baking sheet. Bake at 400°F. 10 minutes; reduce temperature to 350°F. and bake until light and golden brown. Remove to a wire rack. With a small kitchen knife, make a small hole in the side of each cream puff.

Crème pâtissière:
- 1 cup milk
- ¼ cup sugar
- 1 teaspoon butter
- 2 eggs
- ¼ cup flour
- ½ cup cold water
- 1 envelope unflavored gelatin
- 3 egg whites
- 1 tablespoon confectioners' sugar

Combine milk, sugar, and butter in a small saucepan; bring to boiling. Mix eggs and flour together thoroughly in a bowl. Pour in boiling milk mixture, stirring constantly. Return all to saucepan and cook, stirring constantly, until thickened. Place crème in a bowl, cover with waxed paper to prevent a skin from forming, and cool. Soften gelatin in the cold water. Set over hot water to dissolve. When crème is cooled, stir in gelatin mixture. Chill until mixture mounds when dropped from a spoon. Beat egg whites until frothy, add confectioners' sugar and beat until stiff, not dry, peaks are formed. Fold into thickened crème. Using a pastry bag with a small tube, fill cream puffs through hole with some of the crème. Pour remaining crème into center of pastry ring. Decorate with **whipped cream.** Chill ring and cream puffs until filling is set.

Amber toffee syrup:
- ½ cup sugar
- 2 tablespoons water
- ¼ teaspoon cream of tartar

Mix all ingredients in a small saucepan; bring to boiling. Cook until syrup turns a golden yellow. Remove from heat. Holding the filled cream puffs with the point of a knife or a wooden pick, dip into warm syrup. Place on a wire rack. Do not refrigerate them, or the humidity will cause the toffee to melt. Before serving, remove filled ring from refrigerator and stick cream puffs on ring with a little of the syrup. Garnish each with half of a **candied cherry.**   *10 servings*

Sparkling gelatin as we know it today was not available in Andrew Jackson's day, when folks made their own Calves' Foot Jelly. An unusual name by American standards, the term is still used in England and Australia. Anyway, it was a dessert known to be a favorite of Andrew Jackson, often served at his Tennessee home, The Hermitage.

Andrew Jackson's
CALVES' FOOT JELLY

2 cups water
Thin peel of 1 lemon
Thin peel of ¼ orange
¼ cup strained orange juice
¼ cup strained lemon juice
2 tablespoons unflavored gelatin
¾ cup orange juice or pale, dry sherry
¼ cup pale, dry sherry or sack

Place water, lemon peel, and orange peel in a saucepan. Simmer 5 minutes. Add strained orange and lemon juices; simmer another 10 minutes. Soften gelatin in the ¾ cup orange juice or sherry. Add the gelatin to hot liquid and stir until gelatin is completely dissolved. Remove from heat and stir in sherry or sack. Cool and strain through cheesecloth into a 3-cup mold or individual glass dishes. Chill until firm. Break up with a fork before serving if used in compotes. Add **flavored whipped cream.** *About 6 servings*

Calvin Coolidge's
FAVORITE COOKIES

1½ cups seedless raisins, chopped
½ cup sugar
1 tablespoon all-purpose flour
½ cup water
½ cup butter
½ teaspoon vanilla extract
1 cup sugar
1 egg
3½ cups sifted all-purpose flour
2 teaspoons cream of tartar
1 teaspoon baking soda
½ cup milk
1 egg white for glaze

To make the filling, combine chopped raisins, a mixture of ½ cup sugar and 1 tablespoon flour, and ½ cup water; cook and stir until it thickens. Meanwhile, cream together butter, vanilla extract, and sugar; beat in the egg. Sift dry ingredients and add alternately with milk to the creamed mixture. Blend well after each addition. Roll dough ⅛ inch thick on a floured pastry canvas. Cut with a 2-inch round cookie cutter. Place on greased cookie sheet, add 1 teaspoon raisin filling and cover with another round of cookie dough. Press together with tines of a fork. Brush tops with beaten egg white and bake at 400°F. about 15 minutes.

1½ pounds or 3 dozen cookies

On Nov. 8, 1960, Kennedy defeated the Republican nominee, Vice President Richard M. Nixon, to become the youngest President elected in U.S. history.

John Fitzgerald Kennedy was born on May 29, 1917, at Brookline, a suburb of Boston. His parents, Joseph P. and Rose Fitzgerald Kennedy, were descendants of Irish immigrants. Both his grandfathers had been active in Massachusetts political life.

35TH PRESIDENT
1961-1963

Among William Mount's paintings of life among his farmer neighbors on Long Island in the 19th century is this lively "Rustic Dance After a Sleigh Ride" painted during the Jacksonian era.

Other famous old-time desserts in colonial America were Floating Island, Fools, Flummeries, and Syllabubs. These desserts were as delightful as their names, and, of course, most were English in origin.

OLD FASHIONED "WHIPT" SYLLABUB

    Pound cake
¼ cup water
¾ tablespoon Kirschwasser
1 tablespoon sugar
½ teaspoon unflavored gelatin
1 tablespoon water
¼ cup dry white wine
3 cups whipped cream
1 tablespoon grated lemon peel
    White grapes

Cut four circles, about 1¼ inches in diameter, from ½-inch slices of pound cake. Soak circles in a syrup made by mixing the ¼ cup water, Kirschwasser, and sugar and stirring until sugar is dissolved. Soften gelatin in the 1 tablespoon water. Place over hot water and stir until dissolved. Stir in the wine. Put soaked cake circles into long-stemmed glasses. Combine whipped cream, grated lemon peel, and gelatin-wine mixture. Spoon into glasses on top of cake circles. Chill. Garnish with white grapes to serve.   *4 servings*

Here is a rich dessert that tops a light meal or is just right for a bridge party.

AMBROSIAL BRIDGE DESSERT

½ pound butter, softened
1¼ cups sugar
½ quart strawberries, washed, hulled, and quartered (reserve a few whole berries for garnish)
½ cup broken pecan meats
2 egg whites
    Vanilla wafers, finely crushed
    Whipped cream

Cream butter and sugar until extra smooth. Mix in strawberries and pecans. Fold in egg whites beaten until stiff, not dry, peaks are formed. Lightly butter an 8 x 8 x 2-inch glass baking dish. Line dish with crushed wafers; add a layer of strawberry mixture. Continue to alternate layers, ending with crushed wafers. Chill 12 hours or overnight. Cut into squares to serve. Top with whipped cream and a garnish of whole strawberries.   *6 to 8 servings*

36TH PRESIDENT
1963-1969

Just like Kennedy's Fish Chowder and Eisenhower's Beef Stew, a couple of decades ago everyone wanted the recipe for Mrs. Truman's homey Ozark Pudding. Here it is again, an easy but quite satisfactory and tasty dessert.

Mrs. Harry Truman's
OZARK PUDDING

- 1 egg
- ¾ cup sugar
- ¼ cup all-purpose flour
- 1¼ teaspoons baking powder
- ⅛ teaspoon salt
- ½ cup chopped nuts
- ½ cup chopped apple
- 1 teaspoon vanilla extract

Beat together egg and sugar until thoroughly blended and smooth. Blend flour, baking powder, and salt; mix into the egg-sugar mixture. Stir in chopped nuts, chopped apple, and vanilla extract. Turn into a greased 8-inch pie pan. Bake at 350°F. about 35 minutes. Serve warm or cold with **whipped cream** or **ice cream.**

6 servings

This is an authentic recipe for Teddy Roosevelt's favorite cookie, a delicious buttery treat especially popular with the entire family at yule.

Teddy Roosevelt's
PHILADELPHIA SAND TARTS

- 1 cup butter
- 2 teaspoons vanilla extract
- 2 cups sugar
- 2 eggs
- 1 egg, separated
- 4 cups sifted all-purpose flour
- Sugar and cinnamon

Cream butter and vanilla extract. Gradually add sugar, beating constantly until light and fluffy. Add eggs, one at a time, beating well after each addition. Beat in the egg yolk, then blend in the flour. Mix well. Chill if necessary. Roll thin on a lightly floured surface, cut with a round cookie cutter 2½ inches in diameter, and brush with remaining egg white, slightly beaten. Sprinkle with sugar and cinnamon. Place on greased cookie sheets and bake at 350°F. 8 to 10 minutes.

About 6 dozen cookies

Jumbles are among our earliest sugar cookies. A recipe for "jumbals" appears in The Compleat Housewife, a cookbook published in 1766. That recipe is quite similar to the one used by the Polks. Polk was president way back in 1849. We suspect that Mrs. Polk used rose water (you can get it at your pharmacy) in place of wine when she was making jumbles, for Mrs. Polk was a temperance woman and opposed to all forms of alcohol and dancing. This recipe is from the Polk homestead in Columbia, Tennessee.

President Polk's
FAVORITE JUMBLES

¾ pound butter
1 pound (2 cups) sugar
4 egg yolks
2 egg whites, beaten
1 wine glass rose water or wine (½ cup)
1½ pounds (6 cups) sifted all-purpose
    flour

Cream butter and sugar together. Beat in egg yolks, egg whites, and rose water or wine. Stir in flour. Roll out mixture to ¼-inch thickness. (Although Polk's recipe did not call for this, sometimes it is easier to handle dough if it is chilled a few minutes before being rolled out.) Cut into shapes. Brush with beaten **egg white,** sprinkle with **confectioners' sugar** and bake at 375°F. 20 minutes. *About 12 dozen cookies*

Sorbet was the name of the original iced dessert that so delighted Americans in the Victorian age. It was always eaten in the middle of a large meal as, believe it or not, an aid to digestion. This is not too difficult to believe when you consider that banquet menus of the Victorian-age Presidents (Grant's for one) ran to as heavy as 29 courses! Frozen punches, pureed fruits, often liquors, were the ingredients of sorbets. Punch au Kirsch was included in the state dinner Rutherford B. Hayes gave in honor of his Imperial Highness, the Grand Duke Alexis Alexandrovich, of Russia. The dinner

was held at 7 P.M. Thursday, April 19, 1877, at The Executive Mansion. It was the only time Mrs. Hayes, a temperance woman, ever allowed liquor to be served in any way. Punch au Kirsch Sorbet was served after the 36 selected guests had consumed Consommé Printanier a la Royale, plus stuffed bass, filet mignon, chicken volaille, lamb chops, pigeons, and a side dish of foie gras. After the sorbet came potatoes, asparagus, a cheese casserole, salad, cherry crèmes, fruit-flavored gelatins, desserts, and coffee.

Sorbets are not to be served firm like sherbets. Rather, the consistency is creamy and mushy, almost drinkable by the time one is finished. Serve in stemware, if possible—goblets, parfaits, saucer champagnes, or even pilsner glasses.

BANANA SORBET

1 egg white
1 cup sugar
¼ cup orange juice
2 tablespoons lemon juice
2 ripe bananas (with brown-flecked peel),
    mashed
1 cup water

Beat egg white with rotary or electric beater until frothy; gradually add sugar, beating constantly until stiff peaks are formed. Beat in the juices, then mashed banana and the water. When thoroughly blended, turn mixture into a refrigerator tray and freeze until almost firm. Remove from tray and beat until creamy smooth and mushy. Spoon into prechilled stemware. Serve immediately. *About 1½ pints sorbet*

CRANBERRY SORBET

1 pound cranberries
1½ cups water
1 teaspoon lemon-flavored gelatin
2 tablespoons boiling water
¼ cup fresh orange juice
1¼ cups sugar

Rinse cranberries, remove stems, and discard imperfect berries. Cook cranberries in water until they are mushy. Put through a food mill; set aside to cool slightly. Dissolve gelatin in the boiling water. Add orange juice. Stir sugar and orange juice mixture into pureed cranberries. Pour into refrigerator tray. Freeze until almost firm. Remove from tray and beat until creamy smooth and mushy. Spoon into chilled stemware. Serve immediately. *About 1 quart sorbet*

Richard Milhous Nixon was born Jan. 9, 1913, Yorba Linda, California. In 1950 Nixon was elected to the Senate from California. In 1952 he became vice-president of the United States in the Republican landslide that elected Dwight D. Eisenhower president. He was re-elected in 1956.

37TH PRESIDENT

1969-

Nixon visited 56 countries on good-will trips. When Nixon opened the American National Exhibit in Moscow in 1958 he engaged in the vigorous "kitchen debate" with Nikita Khrushchev of the U.S.S.R.

Not all White House desserts of the Kennedys were complicated and difficult to serve. Ice cream and ices were enjoyed by the family and served often. A simple refrigerator dessert enjoyed by Mrs. Kennedy is her Lemon Ice, generally garnished with fresh strawberries. It is interesting to compare her recipe with a Lemon Ice favorite of another first lady, Mrs. Rutherford B. Hayes, who preceded Mrs. Kennedy into the White House by some 84 years.

Jacqueline Kennedy's
LEMON ICE

- 1 quart water
- 3½ cups sugar
- 1 tablespoon grated lemon peel
- 1 cup lemon juice
- Fresh strawberries

Mix water and sugar in a saucepan; bring to boiling and boil 5 minutes. Cool. Stir in lemon peel and juice. Pour into two refrigerator trays and freeze until mushy. Turn into a chilled bowl. Quickly beat with a rotary beater until smooth. Return to trays and freeze again until mushy. Turn mixture into a chilled bowl for a second time and beat until smooth. Return to trays and freeze until firm, about 2 hours. Garnish each serving with strawberries.

About 1½ quarts ice

In making Mrs. Hayes' Lemon Ice, it was necessary to substitute modern day sugar for her "loaf sugar," which was very coarse and amber in color. If you have an ice cream freezer, this recipe can be fun. And you can't beat the fresh lemon flavor.

Mrs. Rutherford B. Hayes'
LEMON ICE

- 6 cups water
- 4½ cups sugar
- Peel from 4 lemons, cut in very thin strips (use only the yellow part, the white is bitter)
- 1¼ cups lemon juice
- 4 egg whites

Boil water and sugar in a saucepan until it is reduced to about 1 quart liquid, skimming if necessary. Cool. When cooled, add lemon peel and juice. Let it infuse for an hour. Strain into freezer trays and freeze until it begins to set. Turn into a chilled bowl. Beat egg whites until stiff, not dry, peaks are formed. Fold into lemon mixture. Turn into a 1½-quart mold and freeze until firm. After addition of egg whites, ice may be frozen in lemon shells. Cut a neat slice from the pointed end of each lemon. Cut a thin slice from the opposite end so that lemons will stand upright. Carefully remove pulp and juice. Fill shells with lemon ice and replace tops. Freeze.

About 1½ quarts ice

Index

HAM MOUSSE
(serves 4 to 6)

½ cup cooked ham (finely ground) 1 cup beef consomme
1 cup tomato juice ½ tsp. paprika

— Mix together and bring to a boil —
4 tbsp. cold water
1 envelope gelatin

Dissolve gelatin in water, add to ham mixture. Put into refrigerator to cool, stirring occasionally. When it begins to slightly congeal, fold in 2 cups whipping cream—whipped until it stands. Add salt to taste. Pour into one large mold or individual molds. Let set in refrigerator until firm. Unmold, garnish with watercress. Serve with mayonnaise thinned with a few drops of lemon juice and a little heavy cream, adding finely chopped chives.

PUMPKIN PIE
(Serves 8)

1 partially baked 10-inch crust 1 (1 lb.) can pumpkin
1-1/4 cups sugar 4 eggs
5 tablespoons plus 1 teaspoon 3 cups milk
   flour 1-1/4 teaspoon vanilla
pinch salt 1 tablespoon molasses
1/2 teaspoon allspice 2 tablespoons plus 2 tea-
1/3 teaspoon ginger   spoons melted butter

Line the unbaked pie crust with brown paper to come up above the sides. Fill the center with uncooked rice or beans (something to weight it down) and bake the crust for 15 minutes at 375 degrees. Meanwhile blend the sugar, flour, salt, allspice and ginger. Stir in the pumpkin and beat in the eggs. Blend the milk and vanilla thoroughly into the mixture and stir in the molasses and melted butter. Remove the paper and rice from the pie shell and pour in the pumpkin filling. Bake at 375 degrees for about 40 minutes, until the custard is set.

White House recipes selected by Mrs. Richard M. Nixon

BARBECUED CHICKEN

Two small chickens cut into halves.
To ½ cup melted butter, add the following:

Juice of **two** lemons
1 tsp. garlic salt
1 tbsp. paprika
1 tbsp. oregano
salt and pepper to taste

Marinate chicken for three to four hours in sauce.
Barbecue—basting often with remainder of sauce—
Or bake—oven at 325—bake 45 minutes—basting often.
Serves four.

HOT CHICKEN SALAD

4 cups cold cut up chicken 2 cups chopped celery
   chunks (cooked) 4 hard cooked eggs (sliced)
2 tbsp. lemon juice 3/4 cup cream of chicken
2/3 cup finely chopped toasted   soup
   almonds 1 tsp. onion finely minced
3/4 cup mayonnaise 2 pimentos cut fine
1 tsp. salt 1-1/2 cups crushed potato
1/2 tsp. monosodium glutamate   chips
1 cup cheese grated

Combine all except cheese and potato chips and almonds. Place in a large rectangular dish. Top with cheese and potato chips and almonds. Let stand overnight in refrigerator. Bake in 400 degree oven for 20 to 25 minutes. Serves 8.